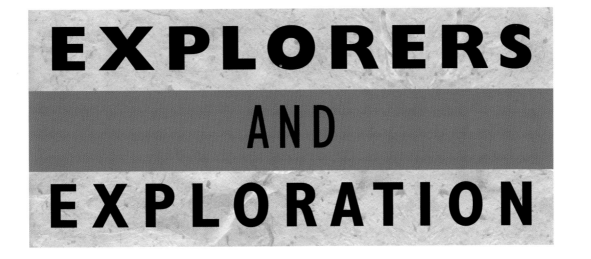

EXPLORERS AND EXPLORATION

BELLINGSHAUSEN, FABIAN GOTTLIEB VON – CHAMPLAIN, SAMUEL DE

Marshall Cavendish
New York • London • Singapore

Marshall Cavendish
99 White Plains Road
Tarrytown, New York 10591-9001

www.marshallcavendish.com

Consultants: Ralph Ehrenberg, former chief, Geography and Map Division, Library of Congress, Washington, DC; Conrad Heidenreich, former historical geography professor, York University, Toronto; Shane Winser, information officer, Royal Geographical Society, London

Contributing authors: Dale Anderson, Kay Barnham, Peter Chrisp, Richard Dargie, Paul Dowswell, Elizabeth Gogerly, Steven Maddocks, John Malam, Stewart Ross, Shane Winser

MARSHALL CAVENDISH
Editor: Thomas McCarthy
Editorial Director: Paul Bernabeo
Production Manager: Michael Esposito

WHITE-THOMSON PUBLISHING
Editors: Alex Woolf and Steven Maddocks
Design: Ross George and Derek Lee
Cartographer: Peter Bull Design
Picture Research: Glass Onion Pictures
Indexer: Fiona Barr

ISBN 0-7614-7535-4 (set)
ISBN 0-7614-7537-0 (vol. 2)

Printed in China

08 07 06 05 04 5 4 3 2 1

Library of Congress Cataloging-in-Publication Data
Explorers and exploration.
   p. cm.
  Includes bibliographical references (p.) and index.
  ISBN 0-7614-7535-4 (set : alk. paper) -- ISBN 0-7614-7536-2 (v. 1) -- ISBN 0-7614-7537-0 (v. 2) -- ISBN 0-7614-7538-9 (v. 3) -- ISBN 0-7614-7539-7 (v. 4) -- ISBN 0-7614-7540-0 (v. 5) -- ISBN 0-7614-7541-9 (v. 6) -- ISBN 0-7614-7542-7 (v. 7) -- ISBN 0-7614-7543-5 (v. 8) -- ISBN 0-7614-7544-3 (v. 9) -- ISBN 0-7614-7545-1 (v. 10) -- ISBN 0-7614-7546-X (v. 11)
  1. Explorers--Encyclopedias. 2. Discoveries in geography--Encyclopedias. I. Marshall Cavendish Corporation. II. Title.
  G80.E95 2005
  910'.92'2--dc22

          2004048292

ILLUSTRATION CREDITS

AKG London: 96, 98, 104 (British Library, London), 121, 126 (Cameraphoto), 135 (Coll. Archiv f. Kunst & Geschichte, Berlin), 140 (Jürgen Sorges), 154 (British Library, London).

Bridgeman Art Library: 89, 91, 94 (Massachusetts Historical Society, Boston), 95 (Washington University, St. Louis, MO), 97 (Archives Charmet), 100 (Kress Collection, Washing3ton, DC), 105, 110, 112, 113, 114 (Collection of Andrew McIntosh Patrick, UK), 127 (Bristol City Museum and Art Gallery, UK), 129 (Library of Congress, Washington, DC), 130, 131 (Bristol City Museum and Art Gallery, UK), 133, 141 (Chris Beetles Ltd., London), 143, 152 (Archives Charmet).

Corbis: 90 (Pat O'Hara), 102 (Kennan Ward), 108 (Lowell Georgia), 138 (Richard Cummins), 139 (Yann Arthus-Bertrand), 142 (Michael S. Lewis), 150 (Wolfgang Kaehler), 158 (James P. Blair).

C. E. Heidenreich: 151 (Library and Archives of Canada, Ottawa), 153 (Musée Condé, Chantilly, France), 155, 156, 157 (Library and Archives of Canada, Ottawa).

Jersey Heritage Trust: 148.

Marin History Museum, San Rafael, CA: 101.

Mary Evans Picture Library: 99, 109, 118, 119, 132, 144.

Peter Newark American Pictures: 107, 122, 124, 136, 145.

Royal Geographical Society: 92 (I. L. Bishop), 93 (I. L. Bishop), 116.

Scott Polar Research Institute: 84.

Topham Picturepoint: 87, 90, 146.

Cover: Copper astrolabe, ninth century (AKG London).

color key	time period
————	to 500
————	500–1400
————	1400–1850
————	1850–1945
————	1945–2000
————	general articles

CONTENTS

BELLINGSHAUSEN, FABIAN GOTTLIEB VON   **84**

BERING, VITUS JONASSEN   **87**

BISHOP, ISABELLA LUCY   **91**

BOONE, DANIEL   **94**

BOUGAINVILLE, LOUIS-ANTOINE DE   **97**

BOYD, LOUISE ARNER   **101**

BRENDAN   **104**

BRIDGER, JIM   **107**

BURKE, ROBERT O'HARA   **110**

BURTON, RICHARD FRANCIS   **113**

BYRD, RICHARD E.   **118**

CABEZA DE VACA, ÁLVAR NÚÑEZ   **122**

CABOT, JOHN   **126**

CABOT, SEBASTIAN   **129**

CABRAL, PEDRO ÁLVARES   **133**

CABRILLO, JUAN RODRÍGUEZ   **136**

CARAVAN   **139**

CARSON, KIT   **144**

CARTERET, PHILIP   **148**

CARTIER, JACQUES   **151**

CHAMPLAIN, SAMUEL DE   **155**

Glossary   **159**

Index   **160**

BELLINGSHAUSEN, FABIAN GOTTLIEB VON

Below **Bellingshausen came from an Estonian landowning family with a tradition of service to the Russian government.**

BORN ON THE Baltic island of Saaremaa, Fabian Gottlieb von Bellingshausen (1778–1852) served while still a young man with the first official Russian naval expedition to sail around the world (1803–1806). From 1819 to 1821, he led a voyage of exploration to the waters around Antarctica; he circumnavigated the continent and may have been the first to sight its mainland.

VOYAGE TO THE SOUTHERN SEAS

In 1819 Czar Alexander I gave Fabian von Bellingshausen command of a Russian scientific expedition whose goal was to "approach as close as possible to the South Pole and search diligently for land." The aim was to discover if there were opportunities for Russian traders and merchants in Antarctica. The Russians were aware that British and American ships sailed to the South Atlantic Ocean to hunt seals, whales, and penguins. Bellingshausen was delighted to be sailing south, for the British explorer James Cook was his hero, and he had studied Cook's journals of his voyages in the southern seas in detail.

The expedition left Russia in July 1819. Bellingshausen's flagship was a corvette called *Vostock* (Russian for "east"), with 117 men on board. The second, smaller ship, the *Mirny* ("peaceful") had 72 men and was commanded by Mikhail Lazarev.

1778
Bellingshausen is born on Saaremaa Island in the Baltic.

1797
Graduates from Russian Naval Academy at Kronstadt, Saint Petersburg.

1803–1806
Sails around the world with a Russian naval expedition.

SEPTEMBER 1819
Sets out from Portsmouth on expedition to Antarctica.

JANUARY 26, 1820
Crosses the Antarctic Circle.

FEBRUARY 22, 1820
Expedition is hit by storms; Bellingshausen heads for Sydney.

JULY–AUGUST 1820
Discovers several islands in the South Pacific.

NOVEMBER 11, 1820
Expedition reaches Macquarie Island to find seals wiped out by hunters.

JANUARY 21, 1821
Bellingshausen discovers Peter I Island.

JANUARY 28, 1821
Expedition reaches Alexander Island.

AUGUST 4, 1821
Expedition returns to Russia after a voyage of over two years.

1852
Bellingshausen dies near Saint Petersburg, aged seventy-three.

Bellingshausen sailed to Portsmouth in Britain to discuss his expedition with Sir Joseph Banks, the president of the Royal Society. Banks had sailed with Cook in the 1770s, and he gave Bellingshausen helpful books and charts of the area. The Russian expedition left Portsmouth on September 5, 1819, and reached the South Atlantic by the end of the year. Bellingshausen mapped the coast of South Georgia and discovered and named the Traversay Islands, part of the South Sandwich Islands group. The ships headed even farther south and crossed the Antarctic Circle on January 26, 1820.

For almost a month the Russians followed the edge of the pack ice around Antarctica. On February 22 heavy storms pounded the ships and forced them to retreat north to Sydney, Australia. After repairing his ships and taking on fresh supplies, Bellingshausen spent a further four months exploring the Pacific, particularly the Tuamoto atolls.

The First Sighting of Antarctica

*T*he thick ice around the waters of Antarctica prevented Captain Cook and other early explorers from getting close enough to spot the continent's landmass. Whalers and sealers were possibly the first to sight the continent, but they left no records. A British Royal Navy officer, Edward Bransfield, spotted the northwestern edge of Antarctica on January 30, 1820. An American sealer, Nathaniel Palmer, also claimed to have made the first sighting of the southern continent in November of that year. However, many years later historians opened Bellingshausen's logbook and found that he had recorded seeing the Fimbul Ice Shelf on January 27, 1820. Bellingshausen and his crew therefore appear to have been the first people to make a definite sighting of Antarctica.

Below **Bellingshausen's circumnavigation of Antarctica (1819–1821).**

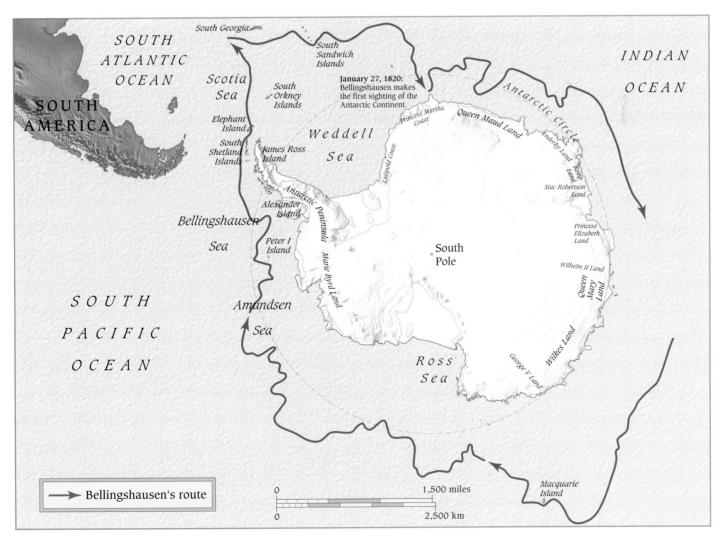

January 27, 1820: Bellingshausen makes the first sighting of the Antarctic Continent.

Bellingshausen's route

0   1,500 miles
0   2,500 km

BACK INTO ANTARCTIC WATERS

In September 1820, Bellingshausen and his crew were back in Sydney, recovering from the rigors of their Pacific voyage and preparing to return to Antarctic waters. In November Bellingshausen sailed to Macquarie Island and learned that sealers had wiped out the population of fur seals. This discovery convinced Bellingshausen that there was little chance that Russian traders would be able to make a profit from seals in the southern ocean.

From Macquarie Island Bellingshausen and his ships sailed south of the sixtieth degree of latitude on one of the toughest journeys in the history of Antarctic exploration. For two months they battled through fog and icebergs on a route well south of Cook's. The *Vostok* was badly damaged and leaked constantly. On January 21, 1821, they sighted land; they discovered Peter I Island and, soon after, Alexander I Island (now called simply Alexander Island), naming them after Russian czars. Bellingshausen then headed back to the South Sandwich Islands. Despite the heavy storms that the *Vostock* and *Mirny* encountered, they became the first known ships to circumnavigate Antarctica since Cook's did so in 1773.

Feeling that the mission was now complete, the Russians set sail for home. Bellingshausen and his men finally dropped anchor at Kronstadt on August 4, 1821. The historic voyage to Antarctica and back had lasted almost twenty-five months. Despite the dangers, only three of Bellingshausen's crew had died.

Bellingshausen never returned to the southern seas but served as a naval officer in Russia's war with Turkey (1828–1829) and as governor of the important naval base at Kronstadt. His achievements in the waters around Antarctica were soon forgotten in Russia, and few Russian ships ventured there

The *Vostock*

*B*ellingshausen managed to get much closer to the Antarctic landmass than earlier explorers, such as Cook. There were important technical reasons for this accomplishment. During the long Napoleonic wars, European shipbuilders had learned how to build heavier and stronger vessels. Bellingshausen's corvette, *Vostock,* was far sturdier than Cook's ship, *Endeavour.* It could therefore make better progress in the ice-filled waters around Antarctica. Bellingshausen knew that the success of his expedition owed much to his ship, and he named Vostock Island in the central Pacific in its honor.

until Soviet whaling fleets reentered Antarctic waters in the late 1940s.

BELLINGSHAUSEN'S LEGACY

When Bellingshausen returned to Russia in August 1821, few people at the czar's court were interested in his discoveries. They saw little chance of making money from the meager resources in Antarctica. The czar even refused to pay for the publication of Bellingshausen's diaries and charts. It was ten years before these important documents were made public. However, others saw the significance of his voyages. The British Admiralty used his accurate charts of the waters around Antarctica until 1931. His name lives on in the Bellingshausen Sea, which lies between the coast of Antarctica and the South Pacific Ocean.

SEE ALSO

- Banks, Joseph
- Cook, James
- Southern Continent

BERING, VITUS JONASSEN

BORN IN THE DANISH SEAPORT OF HORSENS, VITUS BERING (1681–1741) led two important expeditions to the far eastern Russian province of Siberia, where he founded several towns. From Siberia Bering explored and charted the coasts of Kamchatka, Alaska, and the Aleutian Islands. Bering is credited with being the man who proved that Asia and North America were not joined; the stretch of water that separates the two great continents carries his name.

In 1703 at age twenty-two, Vitus Bering enlisted in the newly established Russian navy. He made a name for himself as a commander in the Great Northern War between Russia and Sweden that lasted until 1721.

Below **This bust of Vitus Bering, made in 1991 by Russian scientists, was cast from a wax model that was itself based on the bones of Bering's skull.**

JOURNEY TO THE EAST

In the early eighteenth century, some European geographers believed that Siberia and North America were connected by a land bridge, while others claimed that there was a sea passage between the two landmasses. In 1724 Czar Peter the Great selected Bering to lead an expedition to the far east of his empire to solve the mystery.

Bering left Saint Petersburg in 1725 on a journey across Russia and Siberia that took three and a half years. Once they had crossed the Ural Mountains, Bering and his men waited for the winter ice to melt before rafting along the rivers that traverse the vast Siberian plains. By the end of 1725, the expedition was almost 3,100 miles (5,000 km) east of Saint Petersburg.

The following year Bering moved his men and their supplies another 1,550 miles (2,500 km) across uncharted eastern Siberia. Using sledges and over eight hundred horses, the men followed the tracks of fur trappers through the forests. They endured stifling heat in the summer and subzero temperatures in the winter. Many horses died from starvation and exhaustion.

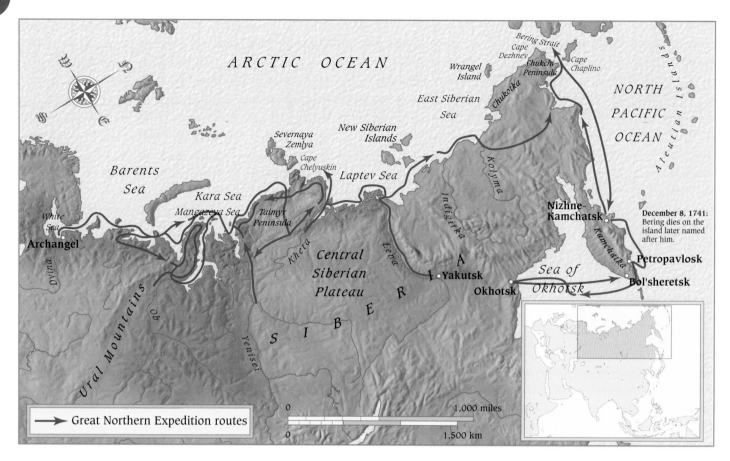

Above **The Great Northern Expedition (1733–1742) mapped virtually the entire Russian coastline from the White Sea to Kamchatka.**

In January 1727 Bering and his men finally reached the sea at Okhotsk, where they found a tiny hamlet inhabited by seal hunters. At Okhotsk, Bering's craftsmen built the *Fortune,* the ship that carried the expedition across to the peninsula of Kamchatka. Bering crossed Kamchatka and reached the Pacific Ocean in March 1728. He built a sturdier ship, the *Saint Gabriel,* and spent the summer of 1728 following the shore northward. On August 27 Bering reached 67°18' north latitude: the point at which the Russian coastline turns west. He had proved that Siberia and the Americas were divided by sea—but because of heavy fog, he failed to see the Alaskan shore.

THE GREAT NORTHERN EXPEDITION

Bering returned to Saint Petersburg in 1730 to arrange another expedition with the new empress, Anna. Known as the Great Northern Expedition, the new project was a huge undertaking. Five separate teams each surveyed 310 miles (500 km) of the north and

1681
Bering is born in Horsens in eastern Jutland, Denmark.

1703
Enters service in the Russian navy.

1725–1730
Leads first expedition to Kamchatka.

AUGUST 27, 1728
Discovers that Asia and North America are separate continents.

1733–1742
Great Northern Expedition maps northern and eastern coasts of Russia.

OCTOBER 1733
Bering sets up expedition base at Yakutsk in Siberia.

1740
Founds the town of Petropavlovsk in southern Kamchatka.

JUNE 1741
Sails north from Kamchatka for the second time.

JULY 16, 1741
Sights Mount Saint Elias in Alaska.

NOVEMBER 17, 1741
Is shipwrecked on island east of Kamchatka, later named Bering Island.

DECEMBER 19, 1741
Dies of exhaustion on Bering Island.

east coasts of Russia from the White Sea to Kamchatka. Almost ten thousand men were involved, many of them scientists who planned to record the animal and plant life they found. There were hopes that Bering would found new settlements and thus open up the vast unexplored region and even hopes that he would find a northeast passage (a sea route from Europe to China).

In June 1741, at the age of sixty, Bering sailed from Petropavlovsk, the small Kamchatkan port he had founded. The second Kamchatka expedition was hampered by poor weather, and many of the crew developed scurvy. Bering's ships, the *Saint Peter* and *Saint Paul*, lost each other in the fog off the Alaskan coast. With its crew weakened by hunger and illness, the *Saint Peter* drifted toward a deserted island in the Commander Group, off Kamchatka. Bering and his surviving crew struggled ashore on November 17.

The conditions were so bad that the men barely managed to dig holes in which to shelter from the icy winds. At night they had little strength to fend off the foxes that bit their ears and noses. Bering died of exhaustion on December 19, 1741. Some of his men survived the winter and built a smaller ship from the remains of the *Saint Peter*. They left the island—which they named after Bering—and sailed back to Kamchatka in August 1742.

BERING'S LEGACY

Bering organized large numbers of men and supplies for expeditions that ranged from the Baltic in the west to within sight of Mount Saint Elias in present-day Alaska in the east. He also founded important towns that were used by later explorers.

Peter the Great 1672–1725

*P*eter was a modernizing czar who wanted Russia to catch up with the more technically advanced states of western Europe. He moved his capital from Moscow to the new port of Saint Petersburg and built the first Russian navy, enlisting skilled Europeans such as Bering. Peter sent several expeditions to explore and chart the farthest, least-known parts of his empire. He hoped that these expeditions would find new, valuable resources for use by the Russian state.

Below **Czar Peter the Great collected a great many ancient objects from Siberia; they form the basis of the collection held by the Hermitage Museum in Saint Petersburg, Russia.**

As a result of Bering's pioneering efforts, Russian fur traders began to settle in the Aleutian Islands and Alaska. However, later Russian czars feared that the British might add Alaska to their Canadian territories, so in 1867 Russia sold Alaska to the United States for 7.2 million dollars. Mapmakers in the eighteenth century marked Bering's achievements by giving his name to the strait and the sea between Siberia and North America.

In 1991 a team of Russian and Danish archaeologists excavated the graves of Bering and five of his crewmen. Bering's skeleton was taken to Moscow, where Russian scientists constructed a wax model of his head from his facial bones. Once the work was completed, Bering's remains were reburied on the distant island in the far north that still bears his name.

SEE ALSO

• Northeast Passage
• Russia
• Shipbuilding

Above **In 1740 Bering's second expedition to Kamchatka entered the Avachinsky inlet of the Kamchatka peninsula, pictured here, where it dropped anchor till spring. It was here that Petropavlovsk was established. Since 1924 the port has been known as Petropavlovsk Kamchatsky.**

Shipbuilding in the East

Thousands of miles from the towns and craftsmen of European Russia, Bering's men had to be able to build and repair their equipment for themselves. Shipwrights and blacksmiths were key members of the expeditions. They designed and built the small boats and rafts that carried Bering's men and supplies down the long Siberian rivers.

Once they reached Kamchatka in the far east of Siberia, Bering's men had to build seagoing ships that could withstand the rigors of the cold northern waters. In 1733 at Yakutsk, Bering founded a town that would serve as an industrial base for current and future expeditions. His men built an iron foundry, a rope factory, and warehouses and thus were able to make and store essential supplies. In 1740 he founded another technical base (at the site of the present-day city of Petropavlovsk). With these factory towns as bases, Bering could explore farther and for longer periods without having to seek help from European Russia far to the west.

BISHOP, ISABELLA LUCY

DURING A REMARKABLE LIFE, the English traveler and writer Isabella Bishop (1831–1904) traveled all over the world. Born Isabella Lucy Bird, she married John Bishop when she was fifty and died at seventy-three, her trunk packed for another journey. Determined, passionate, and independent, Isabella was the first woman to be elected a fellow of the Royal Geographical Society. Her nine books and her photographs of eastern Asia were hugely successful in her own day and continue to be much admired.

Below **This portrait of Isabella Bishop was painted on her wedding day in 1881.**

A RELIGIOUS UPBRINGING

Isabella Bird was born in Yorkshire, northern England. Her father was a high-ranking minister in the Church of England, and her mother was a minister's daughter. Like many girls in Victorian England, Isabella did not go to school, but her parents gave her a thorough education in humanities, sciences, and the Bible.

Evangelical Christianity was a driving force in Isabella's life. She undertook a great deal of charity work in England and Scotland and campaigned on behalf of the poor, whose sufferings were especially acute in Victorian Britain. Later in life, at the age of 58, Isabella traveled to India and Tibet to set up mission hospitals.

THE PERFECT REMEDY

Isabella suffered from a spinal condition throughout her life. When she was twenty-three, a doctor prescribed travel, and so she journeyed to Canada and the United States. The fresh air and exercise did her much good. When she returned, she moved to Edinburgh and wrote about her experiences. A pattern developed in Isabella's life: she would travel, return to Edinburgh to write a book, and then become restless, fall ill, and travel again.

Below **Bishop discovered photography at the age of sixty-one. On her travels she took both a camera and equipment to develop her pictures. This photograph, taken in 1895 in Fukien, China, shows the crew of her boat having dinner.**

WORLD TRAVELER

In 1872 Isabella traveled to Australia and New Zealand. Despite her dislike of the heat and dust and the continuation of her illness, she wrote very favorably about the pleasures of being in the Southern Hemisphere.

The following year Isabella made the long journey across the Pacific to Hawaii in an old paddle steamer. During six months in the Hawaiian islands, she wrote enthusiastic and cheerful letters to her sister, Hennie, in which she described lava fields and active volcanoes.

Isabella then traveled to Colorado, where she spent a further six months walking and riding in the Rockies. She loved the wild life in the mountains and was full of regret as she prepared to make the journey home. "I have cast off my swagger with my spurs," she wrote, meaning that she had left her happiness behind with her cowboy boots.

DARING ADVENTURES

The older Isabella grew, the bolder she became in her travels. In 1878 she visited

OCTOBER 15, 1831
Isabella Lucy Bird is born.

1854
Visits Canada and the United States.

1856
The Englishwoman in America is published.

1872
Isabella travels to Australia and New Zealand.

1873
Sails on to Hawaii and climbs the world's highest volcano, Mauna Loa; later spends several months in the Rockies.

1875
The Hawaiian Archipelago is published.

1878
Isabella travels throughout Japan.

1879
A Lady's Life in the Rocky Mountains is published.

1880
Unbeaten Tracks in Japan is published. Isabella's sister, Hennie, to whom she is extremely close, dies.

MARCH 8, 1881
Isabella marries John Bishop, a physician.

1886
After two years of illness, John Bishop dies of anemia.

1889–1890
Isabella travels to India, Tibet, Persia, and the Black Sea region, visiting areas now part of Iraq, Iran, and Turkey.

Left **Isabella called each photograph "a joy and a triumph."** *Chinese Pictures,* **which contains sixty full-page reproductions with her comments, was published in 1900. This picture shows one of the narrow gorges on the Yangtze River.**

Japan, where attacks on foreigners by samurai (Japanese warriors) were not uncommon. Here, as in all the places she visited, Isabella sought out areas that were untouched, where she could experience the natural world in its purest state.

In 1890 during a trip to Tehran, the capital of present-day Iran, Isabella covered her head, in keeping with Muslim tradition. However, during one horse ride, she removed her veil while enjoying a gallop. Some local men saw her and gave chase, but she managed to escape.

Between 1894 and 1897 Isabella made the longest and perhaps boldest journey of her life, to China and Korea. Suspicion of foreigners was high, and she was threatened on several occasions. Isabella insisted on a boat

"I always feel dull and inactive when I am stationary. The loneliness is dreadful often. When I am traveling I don't feel it, but that is why I can never stay anywhere."

Isabella Bishop (in a letter to Eliza Blackie)

trip up the Yangtze River in central China. The crew struggled to navigate the narrow I-chang gorges, but eventually they reached Szechwan. Isabella wanted to travel farther west, but the party was short of food, and she was forced to turn back.

Writings

Isabella's love of the natural world, her taste for adventure, and her determination to have her way are all apparent in her entertaining accounts of her journeys—particularly in her books about Hawaii and China.

One of her most popular books was one of her first: *A Lady's Life in the Rocky Mountains.* She writes about her guide, a Colorado trapper named Jim Nugent (also known as Rocky Mountain Jim), with great affection. Although there were rumors of a romance, there is no evidence of an affair.

1892
Is elected a fellow of the Royal Geographical Society.

1894–1897
Travels around China, Korea, and Japan.

1899
The Yangtze Valley and Beyond is published.

1901
In her seventieth year, spends six months in Morocco and travels alone in the desert.

October 7, 1904
Dies in Edinburgh.

SEE ALSO
- Exploration and Geographical Societies
- Women and Exploration

BOONE, DANIEL

DANIEL BOONE WAS BORN IN PENNSYLVANIA in 1734 and died in Missouri in 1820. During his life he blazed trails and helped establish new settlements west of the Appalachian Mountains. In the process he became a legendary figure.

Daniel Boone was born near Reading, northwest of Philadelphia. His father was a weaver and blacksmith who also farmed and raised animals. Like other frontier children, Boone had no formal schooling but began helping the family at an early age. By age fourteen he was a skilled woodsman.

Below **This portrait of Daniel Boone, still vigorous in his eighty-sixth year, was painted just a few months before his death.**

MILITARY SERVICE

When Boone was in his teens, his family moved to North Carolina. In 1754 he joined the British forces fighting the French for North American territory in a conflict known as the French and Indian War (1754–1763). In 1755, Boone marched with General James Braddock against Fort Duquesne. The British were ambushed by Indians; though many soldiers, including Braddock, died, Boone, (along with George Washington) survived.

When he returned to North Carolina in 1756, Boone married. He and his wife, Rebecca, eventually had nine children.

EXPLORING LANDS AND BLAZING TRAILS

Though he ran a farm, Boone lived as a hunter and trapper. He spent months in the forests harvesting buffalo, beaver, bear, and elk for their hides. By the 1760s game was becoming scarce, and Boone considered leaving North Carolina. He explored Georgia and Florida and bought some land near Pensacola, Florida, but never settled there.

In 1769 a trader named John Findlay, whom Boone had met on the Braddock expedition, reentered his life. Findlay's travels brought him to North Carolina. He praised

1734
Boone is born in Pennsylvania.

1751
Family settles in North Carolina; Boone becomes a full-time hunter.

1755
Joins Braddock's march during the French and Indian War.

1756
Marries Rebecca Bryan; they settle in North Carolina.

1765
Boone explores in Georgia and Florida.

1769
Begins a two-year hunt in Kentucky.

1775
Blazes Wilderness Road and establishes Boonesborough.

1778
Is captured by Shawnees; escapes and helps defend Boonesborough.

1781
Is chosen to serve in the legislature (lawmaking body) of Virginia.

1788
Moves family to present-day West Virginia.

the virtues of Kentucky and led Boone and four others to the region. Boone spent two years hunting and trapping in Kentucky and, captivated by the good soil and abundant game, decided to settle there with his family.

At the same time, land speculators were attempting to bring settlers into the rich new land. One group recruited Boone to lead the effort. In 1775 he and thirty men armed with axes hacked their way through forests and, by widening an Indian path, created the Wilderness Road. In May they built a fort, which they named Boonesborough.

1799
Moves with Rebecca to Missouri.

1812
At the age of seventy-seven, volunteers to fight in the War of 1812 but is turned down.

1813
Rebecca dies.

1820
Boone dies.

Above **In the 1850s—many years after Boone's death—the American artist George Caleb Bingham painted a romanticized view of the frontiersman leading his family and other settlers into Kentucky. This depiction of Boone, almost like a Moses leading his people to the promised land, underlines the degree to which he had already become a semimythical figure.**

In 1784 a writer named John Filson published a book that included a narrative of Boone's adventures supposedly written by Boone but really penned by Filson. The account established Boone's legend:

Thus I was surrounded with plenty. . . . I was happy in the midst of dangers and inconveniences. In such a diversity it was impossible I should be disposed to melancholy. No populous city, with all the varieties of commerce and stately structures, could afford so much pleasure to my mind, as the beauties of nature I found here.

Soon after, I returned home to my family with a determination to bring them as soon as possible to live in Kentucke [sic], which I esteemed a second paradise, at the risk of my life and fortune.

John Filson, *The Discovery, Settlement and Present State of Kentucke*

Boone Legends

Several legends surround the great frontiersman. One says that he killed a bear in a tree and then carved a description of the incident onto the tree's bark. In the late 1800s someone even claimed to have found the tree, but the fact that the inscription is signed Boon, not Boone, as he always spelled his name, makes the claim seem bogus.

According to another legend, Boone wore a coonskin cap—a hat made of raccoon fur. In truth, Boone loathed such caps.

A third legend suggests that Boone met Lewis and Clark in Missouri as they launched their great expedition in 1804. It is true that Lewis and Clark stopped at the Missouri settlement where Boone and others lived, but there is no record in Clark's journal that they actually met the old explorer.

ATTACKS AND DEFENSES

Disputes in Kentucky between the settlers and Native Americans occasionally flared into conflicts. In 1776 Boone came to the rescue of three girls, including one of his daughters, who had been captured by a group of Native Americans. In 1778 Boone himself was captured. After he escaped, he led the defense of Boonesborough against a combined British and Shawnee attack. The British had joined forces with some of the Native Americans to harass western American settlements during the American War of Independence.

Despite the conflicts, Boone's defense of Boonesborough and the lure of rich land attracted more and more settlers. By 1792, the year Kentucky became a state, more than 70,000 settlers were living there.

LATER LIFE

Boone did not stay in Kentucky for long. He lost his land owing to legal problems and felt the frontiersman's desire to live on the fringes of settled areas. He and his family moved several times until 1799, when he and Rebecca followed one of their sons to Missouri. After Rebecca's death in 1813, Boone continued to hunt and explore and at the age of eighty-two traveled as far as Nebraska. He died four years later, in 1820.

Left **It is widely believed that Daniel Boone was the inspiration for Natty Bumppo, the frontier hero created by the novelist James Fenimore Cooper. Bumppo had Boone's virtues—honesty, courage, and a love of wide open spaces—and appeared in *The Last of the Mohicans* and four other immensely popular novels. In this illustration, from *Leatherstocking*, Bumppo finds a dead Indian.**

SEE ALSO
• Lewis and Clark Expedition

BOUGAINVILLE, LOUIS-ANTOINE DE

LOUIS-ANTOINE DE BOUGAINVILLE was born in Paris, France, on November 11, 1729, and died in the same city on August 31, 1811. Bougainville was the first French navigator to circumnavigate the globe (1766–1769); his book about his travels is considered a classic of its genre.

Louis-Antoine de Bougainville's family was wealthy enough to send him to school and then to university. An excellent scholar, he was especially gifted at mathematics but was inspired to seek adventure by his older brother, Jean-Pierre, who conducted studies into the early history of exploration.

MILITARY BACKGROUND

In 1753 the threat of war between France and Britain persuaded Bougainville to join the army. In 1756 he set sail for Canada from Brest (in Brittany, northern France) on a campaign to protect French land from British attack. For the next four years, Bougainville led his troops with skill and bravery in a series of battles and skirmishes. Nevertheless, France lost the war—and Canada—and Bougainville was transported back to France on a British ship.

BOUGAINVILLE'S NEW IDEA

Bougainville came up with a plan to restore his country's confidence. By gaining control of the Îles Malouines (the Falkland Islands, in the South Atlantic), France would control the passage of all ships that sailed from the Atlantic to the Pacific Oceans. Over three expeditions (1764–1766), Bougainville succeeded in setting up a colony on the islands, to the great displeasure of the Spanish authorities in nearby Argentina. The Spanish protested their case to the French government, and when Bougainville returned to France, he was told that the Îles Malouines had been given to Spain to prevent the British (who also had settlements on the islands) from gaining control of the route.

Below **This engraving shows Bougainville as a French nobleman.**

VOYAGE AROUND THE WORLD

Below **Bougainville's observations of the Tahitians in 1768 were recorded in *Voyage autour du monde* (1771).**

Shortly after his return to France, Bougainville expressed his desire to travel around the world. With the support of the French government, Bougainville departed on December 5, 1766, on the *Boudeuse*. His first stop was the Îles Malouines, where he took part in the ceremony to hand over control of the islands to the Spanish government.

Bougainville spent much of the next few months in South American ports, waiting for his storeship, the *Étoile*, to catch up. When it arrived, the *Étoile* needed repairs. The crew members were involved in fights, the chaplain was murdered, and a number of men deserted. A year after Bougainville left France, the expedition finally set sail on the next part of its journey—through the Strait of Magellan. It took the ships fifty-two days to sail around the southern tip of South America. In January 1768 they finally reached the open waters of the Pacific Ocean.

During their journey across the Pacific, the *Boudeuse* and the *Étoile* stopped at Tahiti. The island's beautiful scenery and friendly people delighted the French sailors. As the ships continued west to Samoa and the New Hebrides, Bougainville claimed several islands for France—some of which he did not even land on. Turning north before he reached Australia, Bougainville traveled via the Solomon Islands, New Ireland, and New Guinea.

By September 1768 many of the crew were suffering from scurvy. Desperate for treatment and supplies, Bougainville visited the island of Buru in Indonesia, before going on to Java, Mauritius, and Cape Town. His last port of call was Ascension Island, where he stopped to collect turtles (whose meat was prized by Europeans as a delicacy).

November 11, 1729
Bougainville is born in Paris, France.

1756
Is elected to the Royal Society, London, for his mathematical achievements.

1764–1766
During three expeditions, sets up a French colony in the Îles Malouines (Falkland Islands).

December 5, 1766
Sets off on his round-the-world voyage.

June 2, 1767
Îles Malouines are formally given to Spain.

March 16, 1769
Arrives back in France after sailing around the world.

1771
Publishes *Voyage autour du monde*.

1772
Tries unsuccessfully to fund an expedition to the North Pole.

1779–1782
Serves in the American War of Independence.

November 27, 1780
Marries Flore-Josephe de Montendre; they have four sons.

July 14, 1789
France becomes a republic.

August 31, 1811
Bougainville dies in Paris.

The *Boudeuse* arrived at Saint Malo in France on March 16, 1769, followed shortly afterward by the *Étoile*.

A FRENCH CELEBRITY

King Louis XV was delighted to see Bougainville, who had become famous as the first French explorer to circumnavigate the globe. Bougainville used his log book and diaries of his adventures to write *Voyage autour du monde* (published in 1771).

It soon became clear that the voyage had not been entirely successful. Although many islands had been located for the first time since the Spanish voyages of the sixteenth century, hardly any new land had been obtained for France. However, valuable scientific data was collected, and Bougainville's account of the Tahitians' way of life influenced many writers—including Rousseau, who described the Tahitians as "noble savages."

In this passage from his account of his journey around the world, Bougainville describes the pace of Tahitian life:

This habit of always living for pleasure has given the Tahitians a marked fondness for . . . rest and happiness. They have acquired within their character a thoughtlessness that astonished us daily . . . nothing interested them; among all the new objects that we gave them, none was successful at keeping their attention for longer than two minutes. It seemed that the slightest thought of work would be unbearable; they would run away from it rather than wear themselves out by thinking about it.

Louis-Antoine de Bougainville, *Voyage autour du monde*

Below **Bougainville and other crew members are depicted crossing the Santa Lucia River (in present-day Uruguay) in a canoe drawn by horses.**

THE FRENCH REVOLUTION AND BEYOND

Bougainville was appointed secretary to Louis XV in 1772, and from 1779 to 1782, he served as commodore of the French fleet that supported the American Revolution. On July 14, 1789, the French monarchy was overthrown, and France became a republic. The following years were difficult for Bougainville; like other members of the upper classes, he and his wife were imprisoned. They were later released without harm (although many others were not so lucky).

Though a supporter of the monarchy, Bougainville also thought that an elected government was fairer. He became a friend of Napoleon Bonaparte, who, on becoming leader of France, made Bougainville a senator.

Bougainville was honored several times in his later years. He received the Légion d'honneur in 1804 and was made Comte (Count) de Bougainville in 1808. In 1811 he died of dysentery contracted during his travels and was given a state funeral. His eldest son, Hyacinthe, continued his father's work and took part in three French naval expeditions to the Pacific between 1800 and 1826.

Above **An 1812 portrait of Napoleon by Jacques-Louis David.**

Napoleon Bonaparte *1769–1821*

Napoleon Bonaparte was born on the island of Corsica on August 15, 1769. After joining the French army and playing increasingly important roles in wars with Austria and Britain, Napoleon's ambition grew. Eventually, seizing the opportunity to lead France as a military dictator, he crowned himself emperor in 1804. An extremely popular leader, Napoleon I introduced a number of important reforms that were to make a lasting impression on France. However, a number of unsuccessful military campaigns, including his ill-fated invasion of Russia in 1812, forced Napoleon I to abdicate. Although he briefly regained power, his army was defeated at Waterloo. Napoleon was sent to Saint Helena, a remote island in the South Atlantic Ocean, where he died on May 5, 1821.

SEE ALSO

• France

BOYD, LOUISE ARNER

LOUISE ARNER BOYD WAS BORN IN CALIFORNIA in 1887 and she died there in 1972. Her expeditions to explore and photograph the Arctic Ocean earned her the name the "ice woman." In 1955 Boyd became the first woman to fly over the North Pole.

In 1920, after the death of her parents, Louise Boyd inherited the fortune made by her father's company. In the following years she used her inheritance to travel in Europe. Then, in 1924, she took a cruise to Spitsbergen, the largest island of the Svalbard archipelago, midway between Norway and the North Pole. This first trip was intended as a pleasure cruise, but it gave Boyd a lifelong interest in the Arctic.

In 1926 Boyd chartered a ship to Franz Josef Land—a cluster of islands east of Svalbard—to hunt for polar bears and walrus. Boyd was fascinated by the untamed beauty of the Arctic. On clear nights the aurora borealis (northern lights) filled the sky with rays of green, blue, red, and yellow. In the summer the continual presence of the sun above the horizon turned the Arctic into the "land of the midnight sun."

RESCUE MISSION

Two years later Boyd chartered the same ship for another Arctic voyage. Just before her departure she heard reports that the Norwegian explorer Roald Amundsen had disappeared. Amundsen had gone missing while he in turn was searching for the Italian explorer Umberto Nobile, who was lost on his way back from the North Pole. Boyd offered to help search for Amundsen; for three months she combed the seas from Franz Josef Land in the east to Greenland in the west. Although she traveled nearly ten thousand miles, her search for Amundsen was unsuccessful. For her efforts, King Haakon VII of Norway awarded Boyd the Chevalier Cross of the Order of Saint Olav. She was the first non-Norwegian woman to be honored in this way.

Below **During the early 1930s, Boyd explored remote parts of northeastern Greenland, where an area was later named Louise Boyd Land in her honor.**

Above **Seeing the aurora borealis fueled Boyd's passion for the Arctic.**

RESEARCH IN THE ARCTIC

Ice covers almost 85 percent of Greenland, and its coastline is a maze of fjords that were carved into the land by glaciers. In 1931 Boyd led a scientific expedition to study and photograph the glaciers along Greenland's northeastern coast. Boyd's work took her to the little-known De Geer Glacier. A small area adjoining the glacier was later named in her honor.

The Greenland expedition was the first of five Arctic journeys organized by Boyd. The photographs she took of these remote areas would help cartographers to draw up detailed maps of the coasts of Franz Josef Land, Greenland, and Spitsbergen.

1887
Boyd is born in San Rafael, a suburb of San Francisco.

1920
Inherits family fortune; travels in Europe.

1924
Takes a cruise to the Arctic island of Spitsbergen.

1926
Makes hunting expedition to Franz Josef Land.

1928
Searches in vain for Amundsen, who is lost in the Arctic Ocean.

1931
Leads scientific exploration of east coast of Greenland.

1933
Studies glaciers above and beneath the surface of the sea off eastern Greenland.

1935
The Fjord Region of East Greenland is published.

1937–1938
Boyd measures depth of Arctic Ocean northeast of Norway; discovers East Jan Mayen Ridge.

1938 she explored the Arctic Ocean to the north and east of Norway. Again her mission was to measure the depth of the ocean, but she also discovered an underwater mountain ridge that stretches between Jan Mayen Island and Bear Island.

During the Second World War (1939–1945) Boyd's knowledge of the Arctic region became useful to the American military. In 1941 the U.S. government sent her back on a special mission. The magnetic field of the earth is strongest at the North and South Poles. Boyd was asked to study the effect of this magnetism on radio communication. For the rest of the war, Boyd acted as an adviser on military stategy in the Arctic. She was awarded a Certificate of Appreciation by the U.S. Army in 1949 for her work during the war.

FLIGHT OVER THE NORTH POLE

In 1955, Boyd declared her intention to emulate Richard E. Byrd and Floyd Bennett, who in 1926 had been the first explorers to fly over the North Pole. She took off from Bodø, in northern Norway, in a DC-4 airplane with a Norwegian crew and returned sixteen hours later. She had achieved her remarkable ambition—at the age of sixty-eight. Boyd spent the rest of her life in San Francisco.

In 1933, under the sponsorship of the American Geographical Society, Boyd returned to the region with a team of scientists and studied glaciers both above and beneath the sea using a sonic device.

Boyd wrote about her experiences and adventures, and in 1935 she published *The Fjord Region of East Greenland*. In 1937 and

SEE ALSO
- Amundsen, Roald
- Byrd, Richard E.

1941
U.S. government sponsors Boyd's expedition to the Arctic to study effects of polar magnetism on radio communications.

1942–1943
Boyd acts as adviser to U.S. government on military strategy in the Arctic.

1948
Boyd's second book, *The Coast of Northeast Greenland*, is published.

1949
U.S. Army awards Boyd the Certificate of Appreciation for her work in the war.

1955
Boyd becomes first woman to fly over North Pole.

1972
Dies in San Francisco.

BRENDAN

BRENDAN, ALSO KNOWN AS BRENDAN THE VOYAGER, was born around 484 at Church Hill, near present-day Tralee in southwestern Ireland. He founded several monasteries, but it is his alleged search for "the land promised to the saints" for which he is best remembered. It was said he wanted to find paradise on earth, a quest that led him to sail into the then unknown Atlantic. Brendan died in about 577 and was canonized (made a saint) sometime during the seventh century.

Right **This illustration, from a thirteenth-century manuscript of the *Navigatio,* depicts Brendan encountering a mermaid—and attempting to convert her to Christianity.**

BRENDAN'S LIFE AND WORK

Little is known about Brendan's life. It is clear that he came under the influence of Christianity from an early age. As a child he was placed in the care of an abbess named Ita (c. 480–c. 570). Ita was head of a community of nuns at Killeedy, thirty-five miles (56 km) west of Tralee. She ran a school for boys, where Brendan spent five years as a pupil. He was taught "faith in God with purity of heart; simplicity of life with religion; generosity with love." By learning these principles Brendan prepared himself for a life working in the Christian Church. He completed his religious studies and in 512 CE, when he was about twenty-eight, he became a monk.

It was Brendan's duty as a monk to spread God's word. Although he worked mainly in the west of Ireland, Brendan, like other early Irish monks, was a keen traveler. Later writers claimed he visited Scotland, Wales, and Brittany (in northern France). Wherever he went, he established meeting places for Christians. About 560 he founded a monastery at Clonfert, ninety miles (145 km) north of Tralee. Clonfert was the most important monastery Brendan established; when he finally died at Annaghdown, Ireland, aged about ninety-three, his body was taken to Clonfert and buried in his monastery.

BRENDAN'S VOYAGE

After Brendan's death, a great many stories were told about his life and work. Around the year 900 an account was written by an Irish

The Land That Brendan Found

*T*here is no historical proof that Brendan made a voyage into the Atlantic, and the story told in the Middle Ages may have been entirely false. Nevertheless, researchers continue to attempt to identify places Brendan may have visited. These include the Canary Islands, the Azores, Madeira, and the Faeroe Islands.

The most startling claim is that Brendan reached the island of Bermuda, the Bahamas, or even the mainland of North America (possibly Newfoundland). If true, then Brendan reached the American continent 450 years before Leif Eriksson and 900 years before Christopher Columbus.

Mapmakers who knew the Brendan story marked a "Saint Brendan's Island" on their maps, placing it far to the west of Africa. Columbus probably knew the story, and it may have inspired him during his voyage across the Atlantic Ocean in 1492.

monk of a seven-year-long sea voyage Brendan was said to have made. The voyage may have taken place between about 566 and 573, when Brendan was in his eighties. The account, which was written in Latin, was called *Navigatio Sancti Brendani* (*The Voyage of Saint Brendan*). Such was its popularity that over the years it was translated into numerous languages, including English, French, German, Flemish, Italian, and Norse.

According to the account, Brendan sailed from Ireland out into the Atlantic Ocean. He traveled in a curragh, a wooden-framed boat covered with leather ox hides, with a band of fellow monks. The number of monks who sailed with him varies according to the version of the story. There may have been as

c. 484 CE Brendan is born at Church Hill, near Tralee, Ireland.	**512** Becomes a monk.	**c. 563** Perhaps visits Scotland.	**c. 577** Dies at Annaghdown, Ireland.	**c. 1125** *Navigatio* is translated into French.
c. 490s Attends a school at Killeedy, Ireland, run by Abbess Ita.	**c. 550** Establishes a monastery at Coney Island, Ireland. **c. 560** Establishes a monastery at Clonfert, Ireland.	**c. 566–573** Is alleged to have traveled across the Atlantic Ocean.	**c. 900** *Navigatio Sancti Brendani* is written in Latin.	**c. 1150** *Navigatio* is translated into German.

Recreating Brendan's Voyage

*I*n the 1970s Tim Severin, an English historian and traveler born in 1940, set out to discover if it was possible to cross the Atlantic Ocean in a boat similar to the one Brendan was said to have used. He built a boat consisting of waterproof leather ox hides stretched over an ash framework and named it the *Brendan*. On May 17, 1976, Severin sailed from Ireland. As he headed north, he realized that many of the landmarks mentioned in the Brendan story made sense, especially from the point of view of a sixth-century monk. For example, the coast of Iceland, with its active volcanoes, may well have seemed like the edge of hell, and icebergs do resemble the crystal pillars described in Brendan's story. After stopping for the winter in Reykjavik, Iceland, Severin and the *Brendan* reached Newfoundland on June 26, 1977. Severin had proved that a leather boat could cross the Atlantic.

few as 18 or as many as 150. Brendan was said to have been searching for a fabled island paradise that he believed was home to all the Christian saints. He sailed for five years among the islands of the North Atlantic until he arrived at a place he believed was "the land promised to the saints." After Brendan had spent fifteen days exploring the place, an angel appeared and told him to return to Ireland.

Below **The story of Brendan's voyage describes his encounter with a friendly whale. Brendan was said to have celebrated Easter Sunday mass on the whale's back, a scene depicted on this page from a 1476 German manuscript of the *Navigatio*.**

et belua in mari que grece aspido delone dicat Aspido ut Laune u aspido restitudo. Oere enam dicta. ob bere unmanitate corporis. est eni sicut ille q egrepu

SEE ALSO

- Columbus, Christopher
- Leif Eriksson
- Ships and Boats

BRIDGER, JIM

JIM BRIDGER, BORN IN 1804, was one of the leading mountain men of the Rocky Mountain fur trade. Through his travels, he became extremely familiar with the trails, rivers, and mountains of the American West and shared his knowledge with countless travelers and explorers. He retired to Missouri, where he died in 1881.

TRAPPING

When Jim Bridger was still young, his family moved to Missouri, then a frontier area. When both parents died a few years later, Bridger began to work as a blacksmith's apprentice. In 1822 William Ashley, a fur trader, advertised in the *Missouri Republican* for "Enterprising Young Men" willing to work in the wilderness. Bridger, still in his teens, dropped black-smithing to sign up as a fur trapper.

Bridger spent the next several years in the fur trade. On his second trip his lack of experience led him to commit a grave error. In the winter of 1824 to 1825, Bridger and another mountain man abandoned a colleague who had been badly mauled by a grizzly bear. The injured man survived and was forced to make a grueling six-week journey to safety. Bridger was forgiven because of his youth.

Over time, Bridger gained skill, judgment, and a vast store of knowledge about the Rockies and Great Basin regions. During the winter of 1824 to 1825, he became perhaps the first Anglo-American to see the Great Salt Lake. He also witnessed the hot springs and geysers in the area that is now designated Yellowstone National Park.

In 1830 Bridger joined with four other trappers to form the Rocky Mountain Fur Company. However, the company lasted only a few years; overhunting had devastated the beaver population of the mountains, and competition from other companies was too tough. Bridger continued to trap, but that life was becoming more difficult.

Below **Jim Bridger, American trapper, guide, and explorer (nicknamed Old Gabe by his colleagues) lived and worked in the Rocky Mountain region for nearly fifty years.**

In the late 1830s Bridger married his first wife, Cora, a member of the Flathead tribe, with whom he had three children. Although he could neither read nor write, Bridger had developed into an excellent horseman and a superb shot.

Above **A restored bedroom at Fort Bridger, now a museum. Fort Bridger was strategically placed to help the wagon trains moving west along the Oregon Trail and the California Trail.**

FORT BRIDGER

Bridger embarked on a new career in the early 1840s. Together with Louis Vasquez, another former trapper, he built a fort. It was not very impressive—one visitor described it as "two or three miserable log cabins." However, it had a good location along the newly forming Oregon Trail (a nineteenth-century route used by pioneers and settlers) in present-day southwestern Wyoming. Fort Bridger stood in a valley with plenty of grass and water just west of a long stretch of desert. As Bridger noted, the settlers who arrived there were "generally well supplied with money" and "in want of all kinds of supplies."

Bridger carried on brisk business supplying the wagon trains and trading with local American Indians. Calling on his vast knowledge of the mountains, he gave travelers advice on what routes to follow.

Bridger's first wife died in 1846. In 1848 he married a Ute woman, who died in childbirth the following year. In 1850 he married a Shoshone woman, who had two children with him. He had all his children educated at missionary schools.

SCOUT AND GUIDE

In the 1840s Mormons settled near Bridger's fort. Bridger and the Mormons did not get along. The Mormons bought the fort in 1855, but Bridger harbored ill feelings toward them. A few years later the U.S. government sent troops to punish the Mormons for defying federal rule of their territory. Bridger happily guided the soldiers to Mormon lands.

1804
Bridger is born in Richmond, Virginia.

1812
Family moves to Saint Louis, Missouri.

1818
Both parents die.

1822
Bridger joins Ashley's first fur trapping expedition.

1830–1834
Is partner in Rocky Mountain Fur Company.

1843
Joins with Vasquez to build Fort Bridger.

1849
Begins working as guide to government-sponsored expeditions.

1855
Sells Fort Bridger to the Mormons.

1866
Retires to home in Missouri.

1881
Dies at the age of seventy-seven.

The Mormons

Mormons are members of the Church of Jesus Christ of Latter-day Saints. The religion was founded by Joseph Smith in the 1830s. Suspicion and mistrust from Christian neighbors forced the Mormons to move several times. One reason for that opposition was the fact that the Mormons practiced polygamy. In 1844 a mob killed Smith, and leadership passed to one of his followers, named Brigham Young. Two years later Young led a great migration of a few thousand Mormons from Illinois to the Great Salt Lake region. The Mormons stopped at Fort Bridger, and Young talked with Bridger about the prospects of settling near the lake, a region that Bridger praised. The Mormons prospered through hard work. Though the population grew, the U.S. government refused to allow their territory to become a state until the Mormons officially dropped polygamy from church teachings. They did so in 1890, and Utah became a state in 1896.

SALT LAKE CITY—BRIGHAM YOUNG—PROPOSED MORMON TEMPLE.

Bridger took part in several other expeditions, including one that explored the Yellowstone area and another that measured the Bozeman Trail, a trail that branched off from the Oregon Trail and led to southwestern Montana. He also consulted with Grenville Dodge, the engineer hired by the Union Pacific Railroad to oversee the contruction of a railroad line from Iowa to the Pacific. Bridger suggested that the trains cross the Rocky Mountains by using Bridger's Pass, which would lead the railroad along the southern edge of the desolate Great Basin. Dodge eagerly took this advice.

By 1866 Bridger was losing his eyesight. He took his family and settled on a farm in Missouri, where he died fifteen years later.

Above **This 1869 illustration shows Brigham Young, who led the Mormons to the land they called Deseret, the present-day state of Utah. The illustration also includes an early view of Salt Lake City.**

SEE ALSO
- Ashley, William Henry
- Carson, Kit
- Frémont, John
- Smith, Jedediah Strong

BURKE, ROBERT O'HARA

ROBERT O'HARA BURKE (1821–1861) was the leader of the first known journey of exploration to cross Australia from south to north. Although the large and well-equipped expedition attained its transcontinental goal, Burke and two of his men died on the return trip. As a result, Burke's historic land crossing of Australia is also remembered as one of the great disasters in the history of exploration.

Below **An artist's rendering of the departure of the Burke and Wills expedition from Melbourne in 1860.**

Robert Burke was an Irishman who emigrated to South Australia in 1853. Gold had been discovered in Victoria in 1851, and Burke was just one of some 92,000 Europeans who traveled to Melbourne, the capital of Victoria, during 1853.

Burke found work as a police superintendent in a gold mining district. At the time, although Melbourne and other coastal settlements were thriving, little was known for certain about the Australian interior. According to some theories, there was an inland sea at the center of the continent. Other people believed the interior contained good grazing land, a necessity for raising all the sheep and cattle that would be needed to feed the growing number of new settlers.

In 1860 the Royal Society of Victoria in Melbourne decided to mount an expedition to cross Australia from south to north and find out what lay inland. An additional motive was the news that John McDouall Stuart was planning a similar expedition. Stuart was from Adelaide—Melbourne's great rival.

Although he had few qualifications and knew nothing about exploration or survival in the outback, Burke was chosen to lead the expedition, which set off on August 20. The company consisted of twenty men, including a young Englishman, William John Wills, who was the navigator. The men took twenty-four camels, twenty-three horses, and twenty-one tons (19,000 kg) of supplies.

ACROSS AUSTRALIA

The expedition was very large, and its progress was very slow. In order to travel faster, Burke dumped supplies, including the lime juice that would have protected his expedition from scurvy. He also divided his men into two groups. With an advance party of seven others, he traveled to Cooper's Creek, where a base camp was set up. He then divided his expedition again and pushed on with three

men—Wills, Charles Gray, and John King. The others, under William Brahe, were ordered to wait at Cooper's Creek for the relief party.

In February 1861 Burke reached the northern coast and then turned back. Food was now running low, and the men began to suffer from headaches and aching limbs. On April 17 Gray died, and the weakened explorers spent a whole day digging his grave.

Above **The Burke and Wills Expedition (1860–1861). Burke discovered that the Australian interior was a hot, dry, hostile place, with no inland sea or navigable rivers.**

AUGUST 20, 1860
Burke sets off from Melbourne.

OCTOBER 19, 1860
In Menindee, Burke divides his team into two groups and presses on with seven men.

NOVEMBER 11, 1860
Camp is established at Cooper's Creek.

DECEMBER 16, 1860
Burke leaves Cooper's Creek with Wills, Gray, and King.

FEBRUARY 11, 1861
Reaches the Gulf of Carpentaria on the northern coast of Australia.

APRIL 17, 1861
Gray dies.

APRIL 21, 1861
Burke returns to Cooper's Creek to find it abandoned.

c. JUNE 29, 1861
Wills dies.

c. JULY 1, 1861
Burke dies.

SEPTEMBER 15, 1861
King is found by rescue party.

Above **In this depiction Burke, Wills, and King arrive back at Cooper's Creek and are dismayed to find it deserted.**

On April 21, 1861, the party got back to Cooper's Creek, which they were horrified to find deserted. To make matters worse, they found a note from Brahe that said he had left just eight hours before their arrival.

Burke knew that they were too weak to be able to catch up with Brahe. After resting for two days, they set off to follow the creek but found that it trickled out into the desert. While they were away, Brahe, who had had second thoughts about leaving his post, returned to Cooper's Creek. Finding no sign that Burke had been there, he left again.

The explorers were now trapped in Cooper's Creek. They were helped by the local aborigines, who gave them fish and cakes made from the seeds of a plant called nardoo. They also picked and ate the nardoo themselves. However, they did not realize that the seed has to be specially prepared to make it digestible. Wills wrote in his diary, "We are trying to live like the Blacks but find it hard work."

Burke and Wills both died of starvation and scurvy. King was later rescued by the aborigines, who nursed him back to health and cared for him for two months until a rescue party finally arrived.

Burke's Mistakes

The disaster of Burke's expedition was due partly to terrible luck but also to Burke's mistakes. He made no attempt to befriend the aborigines, people who understood the environment and who could have shown him how to survive. He looked down on aborigines and would accept their help only when there was no alternative. By then, however, it was too late.

SEE ALSO
- Exploration and Geographical Societies
- Illness and Disease

BURTON, RICHARD FRANCIS

THE ENGLISH EXPLORER Richard Francis Burton (1821–1890) traveled in Africa, Asia, the Middle East, and South America. In 1858, while on an expedition in Africa to discover the source of the Nile River, he and fellow explorer John Hanning Speke became the first Europeans to see Lake Tanganyika. Burton died in 1890, after a long and adventurous career.

THE MAKING OF AN EXPLORER

Richard Burton was born on March 19, 1821, in Torquay, southwestern England. His father took the family traveling across Europe, and so from an early age Burton grew accustomed to life on the move. Burton had a great talent for languages: while still young he learned French, Spanish, Italian, Portuguese, German, and modern Greek. At nineteen he enrolled at Oxford University, where he studied ancient Greek, Latin, and Arabic. After only a year it was discovered that Burton had been going to horseraces, an activity forbidden to students, and he was expelled.

MASTER OF DISGUISE

After leaving Oxford, Burton joined the army and served in India from 1842 to 1849. For much of the time, he was in the province of Sind (in present-day southeastern Pakistan). His ability to speak the region's languages was put to use when he became his regiment's interpreter. He was also an intelligence officer, with the task of gathering information for his superiors. Burton became a master of disguise, coloring his skin with henna, growing his hair long, and wearing old clothes, all of which made him look like an Indian. For one assignment Burton spied on his fellow soldiers, and he became unpopular as a result. In 1849 he contracted cholera and thus gave the authorities an excuse to send him home.

Left **Richard Burton (top) married Isabel Arundell (bottom) in 1861. After Burton's death in 1890, Isabel burned many of his papers. The loss to history is incalculable.**

Forbidden Cities

For the next three years Burton recuperated in France, where he planned a journey to visit the sacred Muslim cities of Mecca and Medina. Both of these cities, in present-day Saudi Arabia, were out of bounds to non-Muslims. The only way Burton could enter them was to disguise himself. In 1853 he traveled to Arabia, and at the end of January 1854, dressed as a Muslim pilgrim and using the name Mirza Abdullah, he entered Islam's two holiest places.

Mecca and Medina were not the only forbidden places Burton entered that year. He was asked by the army to explore Somaliland in East Africa (present-day Ethiopia and Somalia). Burton was joined on the expedition by other British explorers, including John Hanning Speke (1827–1864). Before the party set off for the Somali interior, Burton went to the slave-trading town of Harer, in northwestern Somaliland, where outsiders were not welcome. Disguised as a local man, he became the first non-Muslim ever to visit

Right **Richard Burton depicted dressed as an Arab. His convincing disguises helped him to enter places that non-Muslims were not allowed to visit.**

In 1856 Burton wrote a 650-page book about his 1854 visit to Somaliland. Here he describes the moment he and his fellow explorers were attacked:

The enemy swarmed like hornets with shouts and screams intending to terrify, and proving that overwhelming odds were against us: it was by no means easy to avoid in the shades of night the jobbing [stabbing] of javelins, and the long heavy daggers thrown at our legs from under and through the opening of the tent. We three remained together; Lt. Herne knelt by my right, on my left was Lt. Speke guarding the entrance, I stood in the centre, having nothing but a sabre. The revolvers were used by my companions with deadly effect; unfortunately there was but one pair.

Richard Burton, *First Footsteps in East Africa*

Below **Burton and Speke's exploration of the Great Lakes region of East Africa (1857–1858).**

Harer. For ten days he explored the town and observed the people and their customs. From Harer he rejoined his fellow explorers, and the party began the expedition into the interior of Somaliland. Burton and Speke never reached their destination: in an attack by Somalis, the two men were wounded.

SEARCH FOR THE SOURCE OF THE NILE

Burton recovered, and after serving with the Indian army in southern Russia during the Crimean War (1854–1856), he returned to Africa in 1857. He had heard reports of an inland sea in East Africa and wondered if it was the source of the Nile River, Africa's greatest waterway. The Nile's source had long been a mystery, and Burton was determined to find it. He organized an expedition, and once again chose Speke to accompany him.

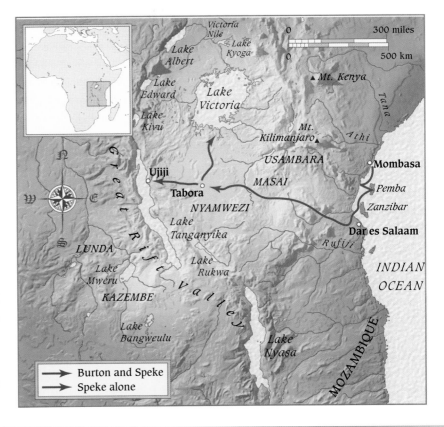

1821
Burton is born in Torquay, England.

1840
Begins to study Arabic at Oxford University.

1842–1849
Joins the Indian army; explores the Sind region of India.

1853–1854
Travels to Arabia; visits Mecca and Medina.

1854–1855
Travels to East Africa; visits Harer and leads expedition to Somaliland.

1857–1858
With John Hanning Speke, explores Great Lakes region of East Africa; makes European discovery of Lake Tanganyika.

1860
Visits North America and observes the Mormon community at Salt Lake City.

1861–1865
Explores Ghana and Congo, West Africa.

1865–1868
Has diplomatic post in Brazil; travels in South America.

1869
Has diplomatic post in Damascus, Syria.

1872
Has diplomatic post in Trieste, Italy.

1877–1878
Joins an expedition to Egypt and Arabia in search of gold.

1886
Is knighted by Queen Victoria.

1890
Dies at Trieste, Italy.

In August 1857 Burton and Speke, served by 130 porters and 30 pack animals, set off from the coast of East Africa. Burton's plan was to travel overland to the source of the Nile's headwaters—something that had not been attempted before. The men headed west for five hundred miles (800 km) to Kezeh (present-day Tabora), where they were told that the "inland sea" was three huge lakes—not the single one that Burton had been expecting. Both he and Speke were weak and suffering from infections, yet they reached one of the lakes, the lake now known as Lake Tanganyika, on February 13, 1858 (the African name for the lake is the Sea of Ujij). Burton was convinced he had found the source of the Nile River, but Speke was not so sure. Speke explored the lake and found no evidence that the Nile flowed from it.

On the return journey, Speke explored an area to the north on his own, while Burton, who was recovering from malaria, stayed at Kezeh. After six weeks Speke rejoined Burton with the news that he had discovered the true source of the Nile—a lake known by Africans as Lake Ukerewe. It was Africa's

Below **Burton and his fellow explorer Speke (both riding donkeys), accompanied by porters, depicted on their expedition to find the source of the Nile River.**

largest lake, and Speke renamed it Lake Victoria, in honor of the reigning queen of England. Burton stubbornly refused to accept the fact that Speke had indeed found the Nile's source, preferring to believe the river flowed from Lake Tanganyika. The ensuing disagreement lasted many years.

BURTON THE DIPLOMAT

In 1861 Burton left the Indian army and went to work for the British Foreign Office as a diplomat. For a man who loved travel and was fluent in languages, it was a natural change of career. Burton's first overseas posting was to an area of West Africa presently covered by Nigeria. From Africa he was posted to Brazil in South America. While there, he explored the country's interior and also visited Paraguay and Chile. In 1869 he was moved to Damascus, Syria (western Asia), and then in 1872 his final posting took him to Trieste, Italy, where he devoted himself to writing. Toward the end of his life, Burton was knighted by Queen Victoria. He died in Trieste on October 19, 1890, aged seventy-nine.

Author and Linguist

A talented linguist who could speak thirty languages, Burton was also a prolific writer. He wrote forty-three books about his explorations alone. After his visit to the forbidden cities of Arabia, he wrote *Personal Narrative of a Pilgrimage to El-Medinah and Meccah* (1855–1856), a study of Muslim life. Following his journey to Lake Tanganyika, he wrote *The Lake Regions of Central Africa* (1860). In addition to his travel writing, which for many men would have been the work of a lifetime, Burton wrote books of folklore and poetry and translated texts into English from many languages, especially Arabic. His translation of *The Arabian Nights*, published in sixteen volumes between 1885 and 1888, was one of the great literary achievements of the nineteenth century, and it is for this work that Burton is now best known.

SEE ALSO

- Livingstone, David
- Speke, John Hanning
- Stanley, Henry Morton

BYRD, RICHARD E.

RICHARD E. BYRD (1888–1957) was born in Winchester, Virginia. As a child he had a particular interest in the Arctic and Antarctic—at that time the last two great territories on earth yet to be properly explored. For his contribution to polar exploration alone, Byrd deserves the acclaim he received as one of America's most admired explorers. Yet Byrd was also a notable pioneer of flight and did much to advance the science of aviation.

Below **Richard E. Byrd in 1930, shortly after his historic first flight to the South Pole.**

Richard E. Byrd spent his entire working life at the cutting edge of his chosen profession. He joined the U.S. Navy but was retired from active service in 1916 following an accident in which he smashed his ankle. He was called up again in 1917, when America joined the First World War, and in 1918 he became one of the U.S. Navy's first pilots. Byrd had a talent for aviation. He developed nighttime landing techniques for seaplanes and pioneered the practice of navigating out of sight of land. His work enabled the U.S. Navy to make its first transatlantic flight in 1919.

In 1925 Byrd directed the navy's exploration of the interior of Ellesmere Island and Greenland. During flights over vast frozen seas and magnificent glaciers, Byrd began to wonder if a flight to the North Pole was feasible. Lacking government backing, he took leave from the navy and set up a private expedition. Byrd had a flair for publicity and making useful friends and financed the trip with funds from such notable American entrepreneurs as Edsel Ford and John D. Rockefeller, Jr. The *New York Times* provided funds and publicity.

OCTOBER 25, 1888
Byrd is born in Winchester, Virginia.

1912
Graduates from U.S. Naval Academy.

1918
Becomes one of the first U.S. Navy pilots.

1925
Directs U.S. Navy exploration of Ellesmere Island and Greenland.

MAY 9, 1926
Makes controversial first flight over North Pole with Floyd Bennet.

1928–1930
Makes first Antarctic expedition.

NOVEMBER 29, 1929
Takes part in first flight over South Pole.

1933–1935
Leads second Antarctic expedition.

FIRST STEPS TO POLAR FAME

Byrd, fellow pilot Floyd Bennet, and a party of newsreel cameramen arrived by ship in King's Bay, Spitsbergen, on April 29, 1926. Their intention was to fly to the North Pole in a three-engine Fokker airplane. By chance, another attempt to reach the Pole by air was also being launched from this location: Lincoln Ellsworth and Roald Amundsen were at King's Bay with their airship *Norge*.

After a dispute with Amundsen, Byrd's men unloaded their plane and took off from the ice on May 9. Fifteen-and-a-half hours later the drone of the Fokker's engines was heard returning to King's Bay. Byrd and Bennet landed, triumphantly announcing they had flown over the Pole. Byrd's fame was assured. He and Bennet were proclaimed national heroes, and Congress awarded Byrd the Congressional Medal of Honor.

Did He or Didn't He?

A great deal of controversy surrounds Byrd's 1926 flight to the North Pole. After his death it was claimed that his fellow pilot, Floyd Bennet, had admitted they had just flown around out of sight of land. Although Byrd's triumph was recognized by the American National Geographic Society, most polar historians now agree that Byrd and Bennet did not reach the Pole. At best, they thought they had, but their navigation records were incorrect. At worst, they knew they had not and deliberately set out to deceive the world.

Below **This montage photograph shows members of Byrd's first Antarctic expedition (1928–1930) and the equipment they used.**

1939–1941
Leads third Antarctic expedition.

1941–1945
Serves as senior naval officer in World War II.

1946–1947
Organizes Operation Highjump, his fourth Antarctic expedition.

1955
Is made officer in charge of U.S. Antarctic programs; returns to Antarctic for his fifth expedition, Operation Deep Freeze.

MARCH 11, 1957
Dies in Boston, Massachusetts.

The flight had indeed been heroic. In those days, flying was quite an ordeal. Both men suffered from extreme cold. They could communicate in the noisy cockpit only by writing notes to one another. An engine began to leak oil halfway through the flight. The compass failed on the return journey, and Byrd had to navigate blind back to Spitsbergen. If the plane had crashed, either from engine failure or lack of fuel, both men would almost certainly have died.

MAPPING THE ANTARCTIC

In 1928 Byrd began a series of expeditions that would secure his reputation as one of the greatest polar explorers of all time. His objective was to map vast unknown areas of the Antarctic, and once again he was funded by wealthy patrons, together with generous contributions from the American public. A large, well-equipped air base named Little America was set up on the Ross Ice Shelf, near to the Bay of Whales. From there Byrd flew over uncharted territory and mapped thousands of square miles, claiming large areas of land for the United States. During the first expedition, which lasted until 1930, Byrd was navigator on the first-ever flight to the South Pole. A four-man crew flew for nineteen hours on November 29, 1929.

International Geophysical Year (IGY)

Geophysics is the study of the earth's physical properties and covers such areas as the earth's magnetic field, earthquakes, and solar radiation. IGY was an international project that lasted from July 1957 to December 1958, during which scientists made a detailed study of these phenomena. Much work was done in the Antarctic, initially under Byrd's direction. As a result a treaty was signed in 1959 declaring that the continent was to be the subject of peaceful scientific investigation.

During World War II Byrd had the vital job of choosing Pacific islands as bases for American forces. When the war ended he returned to Antarctica and supervised another large-scale exploration effort by the U.S. Navy. Called Operation Highjump, it involved thirteen ships, twenty-five airplanes, and nearly five thousand men. Some 300,000 square miles (482,790 km²) of land were photographed, and about one-third as much mapped.

FINAL EXPEDITIONS

In 1955 Byrd returned to the Antarctic for a fifth and final expedition. Operation Deep Freeze was another U.S. Navy exercise; Byrd supervised a series of scientific investigations and journeys of exploration as part of America's contribution to the forthcoming International Geophysical Year.

At the time of his death in 1957, Byrd was internationally renowned as America's foremost authority on the Antarctic. During his extraordinary life he revolutionized exploration of the continent through huge, meticulously planned expeditions and the use of aerial photography. In addition, his achievements in the field of aviation included the establishment of the first transatlantic postal service and the invention of essential aeronautical navigation devices such as the aerial sextant and wind-drift instruments.

Another privately funded expedition, again based at Little America, was launched in 1933 and lasted until 1935. Byrd spent five months alone monitoring the weather in a hut 123 miles (196 km) south of Little America. When his radio messages to base became extremely confused, a rescue attempt was mounted. Not only had Byrd had to endure temperatures of −76° F (−60° C) but faulty heating in the hut had led to carbon monoxide poisoning, which nearly killed him.

Byrd returned to the Antarctic again from 1939 to 1941. This time supported by U.S. government funds, he directed further exploration of the continent.

SEE ALSO
- Amundsen, Roald
- Boyd, Louise Arner
- Ellsworth, Lincoln
- Southern Continent

CABEZA DE VACA, ÁLVAR NÚÑEZ

BORN IN SPAIN around 1490, Álvar Núñez Cabeza de Vaca was one of the first Europeans to explore the present-day states of Florida and Texas. During his extraordinary journey, Cabeza de Vaca recorded valuable information about the peoples, landscape, and wildlife he encountered. He died in Spain around 1560.

Below **First published in Harper's Magazine in 1880, this engraving of Cabeza de Vaca depicts him in the early stages of his remarkable journey through Florida and Texas between 1528 and 1536.**

HISTORY OF A SURNAME

Álvar Núñez Cabeza da Vaca's surname literally means "head of a cow"; according to a family tradition, the king of Navarre honored one of the Spanish explorer's ancestors with the name. The ancestor in question had helped save a troop of the king's soldiers, who were trapped in a valley during a battle, by marking a safe route out of the valley with a cow's skull.

ILL-FATED EXPEDITION

Little is known about Cabeza de Vaca's childhood. As a young man he joined the Spanish army and was part of the expedition led by Pánfilo de Narváez to explore and claim the lands bordering on the Gulf of Mexico (1527–1528). Narváez was under instructions to venture as far inland as he was able. As treasurer of the expedition, Cabeza de Vaca's job was to look after the money.

The expedition set sail from Spain on June 27, 1527, and arrived on the west coast of Florida the following year after a stormy crossing. Narváez wanted to search for gold in Florida. Despite Cabeza de Vaca's warnings, Narváez instructed his ships to continue without him and meet him farther along the coast at Apalachee Bay. Among Narváez's company of three hundred men who went ashore was Cabeza de Vaca, whose misgivings were borne out: when the Spaniards reached Apalachee Bay, the ships, having either landed elsewhere or given the men up for dead, had sailed on to Mexico. Cabeza de Vaca and the others were stranded.

Faced with hostile American Indians and a shortage of food, Narváez now had no choice but to lead his crew along the coast toward Mexico, where he knew he would find Spanish settlers. Illness and hunger killed many of the men, and those remaining were forced to eat their horses to stay alive. They built five rafts and sailed along the coast—and thus were the first Europeans to see the mouth of the Mississippi River. Shortly afterward, the barge carrying Narváez was lost in a storm. Eighty survivors landed on what was probably Galveston Island, Texas, in late 1528. Only fifteen of the party survived the winter, and by 1533 Cabeza de Vaca was one of only four of Narváez's original party still alive. He and the three other "ragged castaways", as they subsequently became known, were the first Europeans to set foot on Texas soil and the first to see bison.

Native Americans in Florida and Texas

Cabeza de Vaca spent eight years in Florida and Texas, during which time he met with several different Indian tribes, including the Cultalchulches and the Avavares, each with a distinct way of life. Some tribes were friendly, while others were more hostile. Generally, they fought by firing arrows with deadly accuracy. The food they ate depended on where they lived; some grew maize, others caught fish, and many gathered plant roots. Life could be tough: Cabeza de Vaca later wrote that food could be so scarce that some Indians "preserve the bones of the fish they eat, of snakes and other animals, to pulverize them and eat the powder."

THE YEARS IN TEXAS

Cabeza de Vaca became separated from his companions. To survive, he traded seashells and mesquite beans acquired from the coastal Indians for skins and red ocher from those living inland. He thus became the first European merchant in Texas. When he finally rejoined the three other Spaniards, they were astonished to find him alive.

EXPERIENCES WITH INDIANS

As they traveled west through Texas, heading toward Mexico, Cabeza de Vaca and his fellow explorers encountered a great many Indian tribes. They could never be sure whether they would be greeted with kindness or violence and were held captive on many occasions. During his time in Texas, Cabeza de Vaca came to believe that the Indians deserved much fairer treatment than they had so far been given by European explorers and traders.

c. 1490
Cabeza de Vaca is born in Andalucia, Spain.

JUNE 1527
Sets sail from Spain as a member of Narváez's expedition.

APRIL 1528
Lands on and explores northwestern coast of Florida.

NOVEMBER 1528
Eighty survivors are shipwrecked on the coast of Texas; Cabeza de Vaca becomes separated from the group and lives among the Indians.

1536
Is reunited with three other survivors; reaches Mexico.

1537
Arrives back in Lisbon.

1540s
Becomes governor of Paraguay; travels overland from coast of Brazil to Asunción.

1542
Explores Paraguay River.

c. 1560
Dies in Seville, Spain.

Despite having no medical training, Cabeza de Vaca gained a reputation as a healer of the sick. After he had prayed for those suffering from illness and applied what little he knew about medical treatment, many sufferers were apparently cured. On several occasions he was rewarded with food and gifts. For removing an arrow from an Indian's chest, he would later be honored as the secular equivalent of the patron saint of the Texas Surgical Society.

ESCAPE

At some point in the 1530s, Cabeza de Vaca and his colleagues were captured by Mariame Indians and held hostage near

Right **Cabeza de Vaca (center) spent eight years living among the native peoples of Texas, during which time he learned their way of life and survived by trading goods between the coastal and inland tribes.**

Cabeza de Vaca's accounts of his travels are full of observations of the ways of life of American Indians and packed with tales of daring exploits. In this passage he tells of his success at treating illness among the Indians:

During all this time the Indians came from many places to seek us and said that we were truly children of the sun. . . . All of us became medicine men, though I was paramount among us in daring and in attempting any sort of cure. And we never healed anyone who did not then tell us that he was well, and they were so confident that they would be cured if we healed them, that they believed that as long as we were there none of them would have to die.

Cabeza de Vaca, *La Relación y Comentarios*

La relacion y comentarios del gouerna dor Aluar nuñez cabeça de vaca, de lo acaescido en las dos jornadas que hizo a las Indias.

Con priuilegio.

¶ Esta tassada por los señores del consejo en O chéta y cinco mrs.

Guadalupe in southern Texas. The men managed to escape and, in July 1536, Cabeza de Vaca and his three colleagues, the only survivors of Narváez's 1528 expedition, finally reached northern Mexico, eight years after they had been given up for dead. Cabeza de Vaca arrived back in Lisbon, Portugal, on August 9, 1537, over ten years after he had first set sail. He described his extraordinary journey in his 1542 book, *Naufragios* (Shipwrecked).

During their time in Texas, the explorers learned much about the people, geology, plant life, and wildlife of the area. Narváez's disastrous expedition had therefore brought some positive benefits.

LATER LIFE

In the early 1540s Cabeza de Vaca became the governor of the Río de la Plata region in present-day Paraguay. During a 600-mile (966 km) journey inland from the coast of Brazil across northeastern Argentina to Asunción, Cabeza de Vaca made the first European sighting of the Iguazú Falls. He also took four hundred Spanish soldiers and eight hundred Guarani Indians up the Paraguay River. In April 1543, while in Asunción, Cabeza de Vaca was deposed and sent back to Spain; his name was eventually cleared. He died in Seville around 1560.

Above **This frontispiece was attached to the 1555 edition of Cabeza de Vaca's *Relación y Comentarios*, in which he described his life among the American Indians.**

SEE ALSO

- Cortés, Hernán
- Narváez, Pánfilo de
- Spain

CABOT, JOHN

BORN GIOVANNI CABOTO, the Italian explorer John Cabot (c. 1451–c. 1498) was the first European known to have reached the North American continent since the eleventh century. In 1497 Cabot traveled to America on behalf of King Henry VII of England; his journey laid the basis for the later English claim to Canada.

John Cabot was born in 1451 in Genoa—in the same place and at about the same time as Christopher Columbus (1451–1506). While

Right **Cabot's discoveries are celebrated in this eighteenth-century painting from his home city of Venice. King Henry VII, as patron of the voyage, stands beside a map of the area of American coast that Cabot explored.**

he was still a young boy, Cabot's family moved to Venice, the principal trading city in Italy. In 1476 he became a Venetian citizen.

With Venice as his base, Cabot made frequent journeys around the Mediterranean and became an experienced seafarer. He also visited the holy Muslim city of Mecca (in present-day Saudi Arabia), where he observed the arrival of camel caravans loaded with rich cargoes of spices. The Meccans told Cabot that the caravans had traveled great distances from the source of the spices in eastern Asia.

Like Columbus, Cabot began to wonder whether Europeans might find a direct route to the source of the spices not by traveling east but by sailing west across the Atlantic. Both Columbus and Cabot had read the writings of the Venetian traveler Marco Polo, in which he described the vast wealth of Cathay (China). Cathay was to be the goal of both explorers.

A NORTHERN VOYAGE

Between 1490 and 1493 Cabot lived in Spain, where he learned of Columbus's triumphant return from his first voyage to the West Indies. Cabot believed that these islands lay southeast of the Asian mainland and decided that a more northerly route would take him directly to the mainland—and to Cathay.

The obvious place to get backing for a northern voyage was England. King Henry VII had already turned down Columbus; Cabot correctly reasoned that Henry would not make the same mistake twice.

In 1495 Cabot settled in the western English port of Bristol, where local fishermen were already making long voyages out into the Atlantic. The following year Cabot was given royal backing for a voyage and was appointed lieutenant governor of any lands he might discover and claim for England. He set out that year in a small ship, the *Matthew*, with a crew of between eighteen and twenty men. Part way through the voyage the ship ran into storms, and Cabot was forced to return.

In 1497 he made a second attempt in the *Matthew*. He set sail from Bristol some time in May, and on June 24 he sighted land. It is not

John Cabot in History

*U*nlike Christopher Columbus, John Cabot was forgotten soon after his death. Columbus had a devoted son, Hernando, who wrote a biography of his father to keep his memory alive. In contrast, John Cabot's son, the explorer Sebastian Cabot, took the credit for his father's discoveries. It was only in the late nineteenth century that researchers, working in the archives of Spain, Venice, and London, pieced together the true story of John Cabot from letters and official documents.

known exactly where this land was, though it may have been Cape Breton (in Nova Scotia) or Cape Bauld (in northern Newfoundland).

Left **This 1906 painting shows John and Sebastian Cabot setting off from Bristol in the *Matthew*. It reflects the view held by Sebastian—that he played as important a role in the voyage as his father. In fact, it is not even certain that Sebastian sailed on the *Matthew*.**

c. 1451
John Cabot is born in Genoa.

1492–1493
Columbus makes his first voyage across the Atlantic.

c. 1495
Cabot settles in Bristol.

March 5, 1496
Attempts his first voyage but is forced to return by a storm.

May 1497
Leaves Bristol in the *Matthew* for the second time.

June 24, 1497
Sights land.

August 6, 1497
Returns to Bristol.

May 1498
Leaves Bristol with a fleet of five ships and is never heard from again.

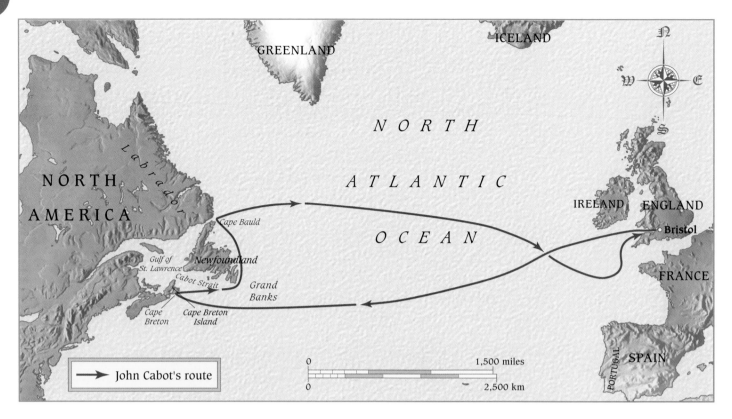

The coastline did not look much like Marco Polo's China, but the Bristol sailors were delighted to see that the waters were teeming with cod. According to reports, the sea was so rich in fish that they could be pulled out of the water in "basket loads." The subsequent exploitation of these cod fishing grounds was to be a major factor in the history of Newfoundland.

Cabot spent a month exploring around 900 miles (1,448 km) of coastline and then returned home. Back in England he was hailed as a hero. He dressed in expensive silks and called himself the Great Admiral. Cabot, whether seriously or not, promised to give various islands to his friends to rule, including one to his Italian barber.

DISAPPEARANCE

In 1498 Cabot set off on a third voyage with a fleet of five ships. One ship, damaged by a storm, turned back. Cabot and the other men were never heard from again. There are clues that some of the ships may have reached America. In 1499 the Spanish explorer Alonso de Ojeda claimed to have met Englishmen in the Caribbean. Two years later a Portuguese explorer, Gaspar Corte Real, visited Newfoundland, where he recovered a broken Italian sword and a pair of silver Venetian earrings. Despite these clues, the fate of John Cabot remains one of the great unsolved mysteries in the history of exploration.

A famed sixteenth-century historian describes Cabot's fate:

He found his new lands only at the ocean's bottom, to which he and his ship are thought to have descended, since, after that voyage, he was never heard of more.

Polydore Vergil, *The Cabot Voyages and Bristol Discovery under Henry VII*

SEE ALSO

- Cabot, Sebastian
- Columbus, Christopher

CABOT, SEBASTIAN

THROUGHOUT THE FIRST HALF of the sixteenth century, Sebastian Cabot (c. 1484–1557) played a leading role in English and Spanish voyages of exploration. The son of the Italian explorer John Cabot, Sebastian enjoyed a long and varied career. He was an explorer, a mapmaker, a navigational expert, and an organizer of expeditions.

Sebastian Cabot was not always honest about himself and his achievements. He took the credit for voyages he had not made and named his birthplace as both Venice and Bristol. Modern scholars believe that he was born in Venice around 1484 but grew up in Bristol, where his father had settled. Sebastian may have accompanied his father on his second voyage across the Atlantic in 1497, when John Cabot reached the coast of North America. Sebastian later falsely claimed to have commanded this expedition, though he had been only thirteen years old at the time.

John Cabot returned from his voyage in triumph in the belief that he had reached Asia. The following year he sailed away on a third voyage, from which he never returned. The shock and disappointment of losing his father at sea did not deter Sebastian from pursuing a career in exploration.

A NEW WORLD

By the early 1500s it was becoming clear that the land encountered by John Cabot was not part of Asia. Amerigo Vespucci, who crossed the Atlantic twice (in 1499 and 1501), described the continent as a "new world"; it was later called America in his honor. For Sebastian Cabot and his contemporaries, America was a barrier between Europe and Asia. The goal of their voyages would be to find a way through or around it.

Left **This nineteenth-century engraving shows John and Sebastian Cabot landing in North America in 1497.**

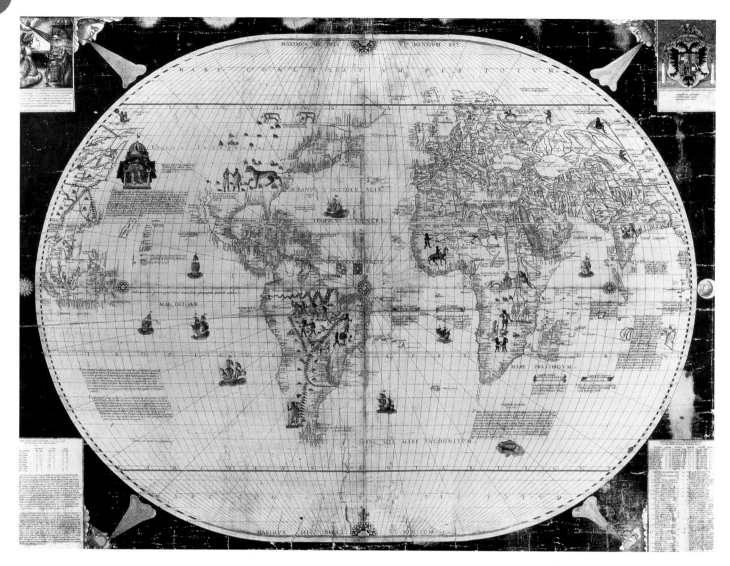

Above **Sebastian Cabot designed this world map in 1544. Cabot's map underestimates the size of the Pacific, shown on the left, even though Magellan had crossed this vast ocean in his voyage of 1520 and 1521.**

Sebastian Cabot's first voyage was probably made in 1508 on behalf of King Henry VII of England. Cabot later claimed that he had sailed with two ships in the hope of finding a northwest passage around America to Asia. He reached the Hudson Strait, where he was discouraged to find the seas full of icebergs. He then sailed south along the coast of America, spent a winter ashore, and returned home the following year.

MAPMAKER AND NAVIGATOR

Back in England, Sebastian learned that Henry VII had died. The new king, Henry VIII, was not interested in backing voyages of exploration. Cabot was forced to make a living as a mapmaker. In 1511 he drew up military maps to assist the combined English and Spanish

force that had invaded France. He was thus given the chance to offer his services to Spain, the country then at the forefront of exploration and discovery. Spain was Cabot's home for the next thirty-five years.

In 1518 Cabot was appointed chief navigator at the School of Navigation in Seville, a position that would have been offered only to an outstanding navigator and mapmaker.

One of Cabot's first projects as chief navigator was to help organize Ferdinand Magellan's expedition of 1519. Magellan took a fleet of five ships through a strait at the southern tip of South America and into the Pacific. He hoped to find the Moluccas (Spice Islands) a short distance away. Instead, he revealed the vast size of the Pacific Ocean, and met his death in a fight. Only one of

Magellan's ships returned to Spain, in 1522, having completed the first voyage around the world.

Under the terms of the 1494 Treaty of Tordesillas, Portugal and Spain had divided the world in two, with the east belonging to the Portuguese and the west to the Spanish. The Portuguese claimed that the Moluccas, which Magellan's surviving ship had reached, lay within their area. There followed a bitter quarrel over the ownership of the islands. Sebastian Cabot claimed to know of other spice islands lying within the Spanish area and offered to lead a voyage to them.

EXPEDITION TO SOUTH AMERICA

During his voyage of 1525 to 1528, Cabot never reached the Pacific. Instead he spent almost three years exploring the Plate River (Río de la Plata) in present-day Argentina, searching fruitlessly for gold and silver. He also quarreled with his officers and made an unsuccessful attempt to found a settlement.

On his return to Spain in 1528, Cabot's voyage was pronounced a failure, and he was banished to Africa. Two years later Emperor Charles V pardoned Cabot and restored him to his post as chief navigator. Cabot stayed in Spain for another seventeen years.

Right **This portrait was painted in England when Cabot was an old man.**

The Padrón Real

*A*s chief navigator, Cabot's tasks were to teach the science of navigation to Spanish captains, to organize voyages, and to question returning explorers about their discoveries. He had to interpret those discoveries in order to update the Padrón Real (Royal Map), the great map of the Indies that was being gradually assembled, much like a jigsaw puzzle. In turn, he used the Padrón Real to make sea charts for the captains.

c. 1484
Sebastian Cabot is born in Venice.

1495
Cabot family settles in England.

1497
John Cabot crosses the Atlantic and lands somewhere in North America.

1498
John Cabot disappears at sea.

1508
Sebastian Cabot searches for a northwest passage to Asia.

1512
Enters the service of Spain as a navigator.

1518
Is appointed chief navigator at Seville.

1525–1528
Leads an expedition bound for the Pacific; explores the Plate River in Argentina.

1530
Is judged responsible for the failure of the 1525–1528 expedition but is later pardoned.

1547
Returns to live in England.

1551
Becomes governor of a company of merchant adventurers whose aim is to find a northeast passage to Asia.

1557
Dies in London.

The ships on which Willoughby and his men died were recovered and brought back to London, where the Italian ambassador, Giovanni Michiel, wrote

[The rescuers] tell strange things about the way in which they were frozen, pen still in hand, and the paper before them, others at tables, plate in hand and spoon in mouth; others opening a locker, and others in various postures, like statues, as if they had been adjusted and placed in those attitudes

Quoted in Giles Milton, *Nathaniel's Nutmeg*

Above **A depiction of Hugh Willoughby and his crew, who froze to death in the icy seas off Lapland (northern Scandinavia).**

IN SEARCH OF A NORTHEAST PASSAGE

Despite his high status in Spain, Sebastian Cabot returned to live in England in 1547. His new objective was to reach China by sailing northeast along the northern coast of Russia. Cabot was able to convince several hundred London merchants to back the scheme, and in 1551 they joined together to form the Company of Merchant Adventurers. Each merchant was to help underwrite the cost of outfitting a fleet of three ships.

Since Sebastian Cabot was too old to sail himself, a handsome and wealthy courtier by the name of Sir Hugh Willoughby was chosen to command the expedition. Although Willoughby knew nothing about seafaring, it was thought that he would make a good impression on the Chinese. Cabot drew up detailed instructions for the voyage.

The fleet, which sailed in 1553, found the route blocked by ice. Willoughby froze to death along with the crews of two of the ships. The crew of the third ship was able to survive by traveling overland to the city of Moscow, where they were welcomed by the Russian ruler, Czar Ivan IV (Ivan the Terrible). Thus, though disastrous for those involved, the voyage was not considered a complete failure, for it established trade relations between England and Russia.

Sebastian Cabot is thought to have died in 1557, probably aged seventy-three, after living through what is still widely regarded as the most important period in the history of exploration.

SEE ALSO

- Cabot, John
- Magellan, Ferdinand
- Northeast Passage
- Northwest Passage
- Vespucci, Amerigo

CABRAL, PEDRO ÁLVARES

THE PORTUGUESE EXPLORER Pedro Álvares Cabral (1467–1520) is remembered as the European discoverer of Brazil. He is believed to have come upon the land by accident in April 1500 when he was blown off course while bound for India. Thanks to Cabral, Brazil is the only Latin American country where Portuguese, rather than Spanish, is the official language.

At the time of his famous voyage, Pedro Cabral was a young nobleman at the court of King Manuel I of Portugal and had never commanded a ship. Yet in 1499 he was made admiral of the largest and most costly fleet ever to sail from Portugal. His was the culmination of a series of expeditions aimed at finding a sea route to India via the southern tip of Africa and thus at winning control of the spice trade for Portugal.

In 1499 Vasco da Gama returned from the first successful voyage to India. He advised the king to send a powerful force to India as quickly as possible but warned him that the Indian Ocean was dominated by Arab traders who would not welcome interference from the Portuguese. Da Gama himself was too exhausted after his long voyage to take command of the new expedition, so Cabral was chosen instead. He took with him Bartolomeu Dias, who had pioneered the route to southern Africa. The fleet consisted of thirteen well-armed ships, carrying over 1,200 men.

REACHING BRAZIL

The fleet sailed on March 8, 1500. The ships headed southwest into the Atlantic, as da Gama had done, to avoid unfavorable winds off the coast of West Africa. Yet Cabral sailed—or perhaps was blown—much farther west than da Gama. On April 21 he sighted land but was unsure whether it was an island or a larger landmass.

Below **This sixteenth-century illustration depicts Cabral's great fleet being hit by a storm in the South Atlantic.**

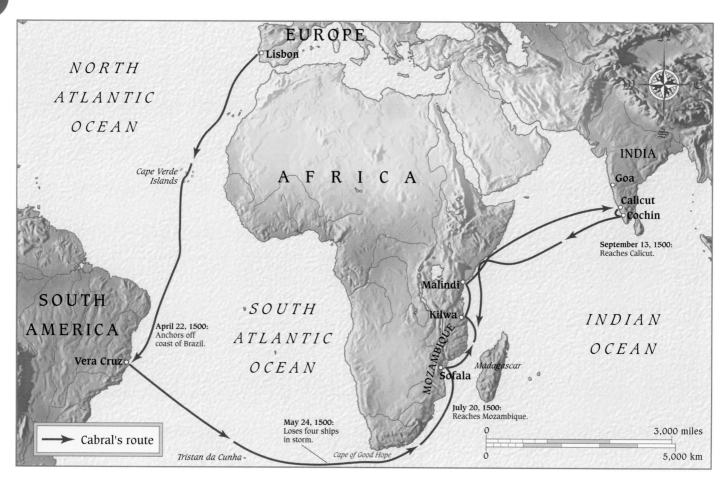

Above **The route of Cabral's voyage to India (1500–1501), the longest sea journey made up until that time.**

The Portuguese went ashore on April 23 and claimed the land for King Manuel. They were welcomed by the Tupinamba, a friendly people whose bodies were painted and who wore colorful feathers. Cabral named the land Terra da Vera Cruz ("land of the true cross"). It was later renamed Brazil after a tree that grew there, a valuable source of red dye.

After several days taking on supplies, Cabral set sail again. He left behind two Portuguese convicts whose job was to find out about the country and learn the lan-guage. As the fleet sailed away, the convicts on the shore were seen to be weeping, while the Tupinamba tried to comfort them. The convicts were never heard from again.

ON TO INDIA

Two ships were sent back to Portugal to report the findings while Cabral and the remainder of his fleet sailed back across the South Atlantic. Four ships were lost as they rounded the Cape of Good Hope, and one further ship embarked on an exploration of

MARCH 8, 1500
Cabral sails for India with thirteen ships; Bartolomeu Dias is among the company.

APRIL 23, 1500
Cabral becomes the first European to set foot on Brazil.

MAY 2, 1500
Leaves Brazil with his fleet; sends two ships back to Portugal.

MAY 24, 1500
Encounters storms off Cape of Good Hope; four ships sink and one is left behind.

JULY 20–30, 1500
The remaining fleet of six ships is repaired in Mozambique.

SEPTEMBER 13, 1500
Cabral reaches Calicut in southwestern India.

DECEMBER 17–19, 1500
Portuguese are attacked in Calicut.

DECEMBER 24, 1500
Cabral reaches Cochin.

JULY 23–27, 1501
Having lost 900 men and seven ships, Cabral's fleet returns to Portugal loaded with spices.

Left **Cabral reads a letter from King Manuel of Portugal to the Samorin, the ruler of Calicut, who listens suspiciously. Misinformed by Vasco da Gama, King Manuel mistakenly believed that the Samorin was a Christian and addressed him as "brother in faith."**

the African coast. On September 13 Cabral reached Calicut in India, a city visited by da Gama the previous year. As da Gama had predicted, Arab merchants were hostile to the Portuguese. Their endeavors to prevent Cabral and his men from trading eventually led to an attack in which around fifty of Cabral's men were killed. Cabral took brutal revenge by capturing every Arab ship in the harbor. He killed all of the crews, sank the ships, and bombarded the city with his guns.

Cabral sailed to another port, Cochin, where the king, an enemy of the ruler of Calicut, welcomed him and allowed him to trade for spices. He returned home the following July with just six of his original ships, five of them loaded with a fortune in spices. However, over nine hundred of his men had died.

Pedro Álvares Cabral never went to sea again. In Portugal he quarreled with Vasco da

A Portuguese official who sailed with Cabral describes the people of Brazil in his May 1, 1500, report to the king:

They seem to me to be people of such innocence that, if we could understand them, they would soon become Christians, because they do not seem to have or to understand any form of religion. . . . For it is certain that this people is good and of pure simplicity, and there can easily be stamped upon them whatever belief we wish to give them.

Letter from Pedro Vaz de Caminha to King Manuel

Gama about who would lead the next fleet to India. The king sided with da Gama, and Cabral left the court to spend the rest of his days in wealthy retirement. Meanwhile, in 1501, the Portuguese sent an Italian, Amerigo Vespucci, to investigate the new lands west of Africa that Cabral had found.

SEE ALSO
- Dias, Bartolomeu
- Gama, Vasco da
- Portugal
- Vespucci, Amerigo

CABRILLO, JUAN RODRÍGUEZ

JUAN RODRÍGUEZ CABRILLO was born around 1500, in either Portugal or Spain, and died on January 3, 1543, on Santa Catalina Island in present-day California. An experienced navigator, Cabrillo was the first European known to have visited California.

MILITARY LIFE

Juan Rodríguez Cabrillo's early life is a mystery, and the identity of his parents is not known. The surviving record of his life begins in 1519, when he served in the Spanish army under Pánfilo de Narváez, who had been ordered to capture and replace Hernán Cortés as ruler of Mexico. (Narváez's campaign was unsuccessful, and Narváez himself, after losing his right eye in a skirmish, was captured and imprisoned by Cortés.) Cabrillo later took part in other military expeditions as

F. GERITZ

Juan Rodríguez Cabrillo

Left **Juan Rodríguez Cabrillo, a Portuguese explorer in the service of Spain, explored the coast of California in 1542 and 1543.**

c. 1500
Cabrillo is born in Portugal or Spain.

1519
Fights alongside Narváez against Cortés.

1530s
Lives in Santiago, Guatemala.

1532
Marries Beatriz Sanchez de Ortega, with whom he has two sons.

1540
Reports on the earthquake that destroys Santiago.

JUNE 1542
Leads expedition to explore the west coast of North America.

SEPTEMBER 1542
Arrives in San Diego Bay.

OCTOBER 1542
Discovers Santa Monica.

NOVEMBER 1542
Discovers Monterey Bay.

JANUARY 3, 1543
Dies on Santa Catalina Island.

FEBRUARY–APRIL 1543
Ferrelo continues the expedition and travels back to Navidad (present-day Acapulco, Mexico).

part of the Spanish conquest and settlement of Central America. At some point he settled with his Spanish wife and family in present-day Guatemala, where he became a trader.

VOYAGE OF DISCOVERY

In the early 1540s the viceroy (ruler) of Mexico, Antonio de Mendoza, asked Cabrillo to lead an expedition north along the west coast of what later became California. The expedition had two purposes. The first was to search for the fabled Northwest Passage, a stretch of water that would provide a direct route from the North Pacific to the North Atlantic and thus make sailors' journeys between the oceans much swifter and safer. (At the time, sailors were forced to make the long and extremely dangerous journey around Cape Horn at the southern tip of South America.) The second purpose of Cabrillo's mission was to search for the fabulously rich cities that Mendoza believed existed along the coast.

CABRILLO SETS SAIL

In June 1542 Cabrillo left the port of Navidad (present-day Acapulco, Mexico); his flagship, the *San Salvador*, was accompanied by at least one other vessel. His voyage was to be brief but eventful.

After he had sailed the length of the Baja Peninsula, one of the first places Cabrillo dropped anchor was a large bay, which he named San Miguel (it was later renamed San Diego). Continuing his journey northward, he stopped at several islands and ports. Among those he named and claimed on behalf of the Spanish crown were San Salvador (present-day Santa Catalina Island) and the Islas de San Lucas (the present-day Channel Islands). His travels certainly took him to Monterey Bay and possibly even as far north as Oregon. In November 1542 Cabrillo's expedition ran into stormy weather, and the ships

A modern historian imagines the effect of Cabrillo's arrival on the American Indian Chumash tribe:

From the shore many Indian canoes flashed across the blue surface of the channel waters, first approaching the Spanish caravels, then circling the gallant flagship swiftly and with apparent ease. Each canoe had twelve to thirteen tanned, muscular Chumash. Most were naked wearing only a waist string, some wore skins or cloaks of sea otter. They were friendly and offered fish to the Spanish. . . . A strange new world had come to the Chumash and though little changed by this first visit, the Indians almost certainly took this event as significant, for the Spanish explorers must have seemed truly powerful to them.

Bruce W. Miller, *Chumash: A Picture of Their World*

were forced to turn back. Later that month Cabrillo arrived back on Santa Catalina Island, where he decided to spend the winter.

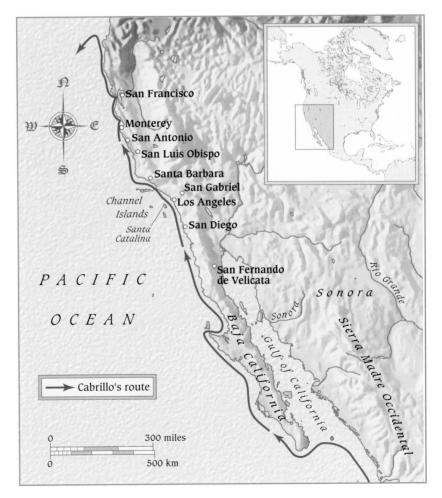

Below **Cabrillo's exploration of the Pacific coast of North America (1542–1543).**

Cabrillo's route

AN UNTIMELY END

When the expedition arrived back at Santa Catalina, it seems that Cabrillo did not receive the welcome he expected. The Native Americans were unfriendly, and the Spanish crews became involved in fights as they tried to come ashore. During one of these clashes, Cabrillo broke his leg. This relatively minor injury became much worse when gangrene set in, and Cabrillo died on January 3, 1543, just seven months after the expedition began.

THE END OF THE EXPEDITION

After Cabrillo's death, his pilot Bartolomé Ferrelo took over as captain of the fleet. On February 18, 1543, the expedition sailed north once more. However, once again they reached only as far as Oregon before stormy weather drove them south. On April 14, 1543, Ferrelo and his fleet made it safely back to Navidad, Mexico.

Even though Cabrillo and Ferrelo had explored the west coast of North America and claimed many areas for Spain, neither was given much credit for the discoveries, and their expedition aroused little Spanish interest. The explorers might have come upon the present-day state of California, but—what was more important at the time—they did not uncover riches or find the Northwest Passage.

Below **This statue of Cabrillo, sculpted by Charles de Almeida and installed in 1949, overlooks San Diego Bay in California.**

A Tribute to Cabrillo

When Juan Rodríguez Cabrillo landed at San Diego Bay on September 28, 1542, he became the first European to set foot on what later became the west coast of the United States. On October 14, 1913, the people of California commemorated his achievement with the Cabrillo National Monument. Perched on the peninsula that separates San Diego Bay from the Pacific Ocean, the monument looks out over the place that Cabrillo originally named San Miguel. A festival is held every year to reenact his historic landing.

SEE ALSO

• Cortés, Hernán • Narváez, Pánfilo de
• Northwest Passage • Spain

CARAVAN

THE WORD *CARAVAN* comes from the Persian *karwan,* meaning "a company of travelers." Since the earliest times people in Africa and Asia have traveled together in convoys in order to protect themselves from bandits and to increase their chances of survival on long and difficult journeys. Although most caravans consisted of merchants trading goods between important cities, some were groups of pilgrims traveling to holy cities, such as Jerusalem and Mecca.

The routes the caravans followed were often named after the commodities traded along the way. The Silk Road ran from China through western Asia to the Mediterranean world; the Spice Route provided a passage to Europe from South Asia; frankincense and myrrh were transported along the Incense Trail from southern Arabia; and the Salt Road ran across the Sahara Desert of North Africa. Along these routes towns and other places of rest, such as oases, were few and far between.

Caravans in the ancient and medieval world were often huge and took weeks to assemble. Muslim records show that caravans of up to 20,000 people and several hundred thousand animals were common on the roads between important cities such as Cairo, Baghdad, and Mecca. Some caravans used wheeled wagons, but they were unsuited to desert conditions. Early caravans also used horses and donkeys, although these animals struggled because of the fierce heat and the lack of forage. From around 1000 BCE the preferred means of caravan transport across the deserts of the Middle East and Central Asia was the camel.

Below **A camel caravan crosses desert dunes near Nouakchott, Mauritania. This mode of travel has not entirely disappeared from the modern world.**

Above **This well-preserved caravanserie in Kyrgyzstan had stone walls to protect the merchants inside from harsh winds, as well as from raiding bandits.**

Life on a caravan was tough. Certain skills were required for survival on the move. Travelers needed to know how to handle animals, how to forage for food, and how to make and repair such things as shoes and tents. Caravan families elected their own leader; they chose someone who had traveled the routes many times and knew the best places to find shelter or to trade.

Caravanseries

The rulers of lands that lay on trade routes realized that caravan merchants needed shelters in which to rest after long journeys in harsh conditions. They built merchants' inns called caravanseries. Often these inns were built at oases or at points where two or more caravan routes crossed.

The caravanseries were cool walled enclosures built around a source of water, such as a well or a fountain. Some had two stories. Animals could be stabled and goods stored on the ground floor, while the merchants could eat and trade in the *manzil* (travelers' room) on the floor above.

Zubayda, wife of the great caliph Harun al-Rashid, built a famous string of caravanseries between Baghdad and Mecca in the late eighth century CE. The later Ottoman sultans also built dozens of caravanseries across their empire. Many of these survive in excellent condition.

The Ship of the Desert

The caravan trade flourished at the beginning of the first millennium BCE, when the camel was first domesticated and used as a pack animal. The camel was the perfect beast of burden on the caravan roads, where the weather was often harsh and food and water often scarce.

The Arabian camel's short fur keeps it cool in the desert, while the longer hair of the Bactrian camel protects it from the colder winds in the mountains of central Asia. Camels sweat little, so they do not lose as much water as other animals do in very hot weather.

The camel's mouth is protetcted by a thick lining, which enables it to eat dried leaves, rough grasses, twigs, and the sharpest desert plants without harming itself. Thick eyebrows shield the camel's eyes from the sun, and special water glands wash out particles of sand. Fat stored in the camel's hump helps it travel for days without much need for food or rest. Most camels can carry a load of up to 440 pounds (200 kg). Depending on the weather, camels can travel a distance of between fifteen and thirty miles (24–48 km) a day. If the camels need extra food, the travelers feed them food that is light and easy to carry, such as dates and seeds.

Below Camel caravans have been a common sight crossing the deserts of the Middle East since the first millennium BCE.

c. 1000 BCE
Camels are domesticated in Africa.

c. 1000 BCE–400 CE
Caravans trading in western Asia flourish under Assyrian and Persian kings.

206 BCE–220 CE
Chinese Han emperors encourage silk caravans to the Middle East.

31 BCE– 650 CE
Roman and Byzantine Empires control caravan routes in North Africa and western Asia.

650–720
Most caravan routes fall under control of Muslim rulers.

1250–1450
Salt caravans between the Maghreb and West Africa enjoy a golden age.

1250–1517
Cairo becomes the center of the caravan trade while Egypt is under the rule of the Mamluks.

1453–1900
Caravanseries are built across the Ottoman Empire along routes leading to Istanbul.

TRADING

To overcome language barriers, caravan merchants on the Salt Road sold their goods in a manner that is known as the silent, or dumb, trade. The caravan would stop at trading places along its route, and the merchants would beat their drums loudly as a signal to any people within earshot that the caravan had arrived. Next the merchants would lay out piles of salt on the ground and withdraw a short distance away. Potential buyers would approach and place gold beside the salt. The merchants would continue beating their drums until enough gold had been paid. Finally, the buyers could take up the salt and vanish again into the wild.

On the longer caravan routes, merchants might carry their goods for just a short part of the way and sell their cargoes down the line to merchants accustomed to traveling on the next stage of the route. Because of poor weather and the constant threat of bandits, it could take several years for cinnamon from China or cloves from the Moluccas to reach the Mediterranean.

Caravans often had to pay taxes to rulers of the lands they crossed. At times, rulers such as the Ottoman Turks and the Mamluks of Egypt controlled a monopoly of caravan goods and were thus able to force up the price of scarce commodities. On long caravan journeys there were also many chances to dilute the quality of goods—by adding base powders to precious ground spices, for example. The goods brought by caravan were usually very expensive and sometimes of poor quality.

Below **Modern-day Tuareg traders travel across the Sahara Desert in Niger by camel caravan to buy salt at the oasis of Bilma.**

THE DECLINE OF THE CARAVANS

From the early period of European civilization, when goods from eastern Asia began to arrive in Europe, merchants sought a sea route to the east, so that the goods might be obtained more cheaply and quickly. For many hundreds of years, there was no alternative to the caravans for Europeans seeking to purchase luxury goods from eastern and southeastern Asia. In 1498 the pioneering voyage of Vasco da Gama from Portugal to India finally established a means by which caravans might be bypassed. In the sixteenth century Portuguese and English ships sailed regularly to East Asia and brought luxury goods directly to Europe. The era of the caravans began to draw to a close.

Some caravan trade has continued into more recent times. In the nineteenth century British explorers, such as David Livingstone, witnessed slave caravans run by Arab merchants in central and eastern Africa. Saharan traders still transport salt by camel along the ancient routes, although commodities such as water and petrol tend to be transported across the desert by truck.

Above **In the Middle Ages, Timbuktu in Mali, West Africa, grew into a rich city thanks to markets that traded in slaves, salt, and gold.**

Mansa Musa DIED C. 1332

Mansa Musa became king of the Saharan kingdom of Mali in 1312 CE. A devout Muslim who understood the importance of trade, he tightened Mali's control over the caravan routes between the gold mines in Ghana to the south and the salt-rich lands to the north. He built caravanseries at key points in his kingdom and rooted out bandits who preyed on the caravans. During his reign his capital, Timbuktu, grew into a very wealthy city. Caravans bearing gold, salt, ivory, slaves, and other luxuries poured into this great meeting place in the Sahara.

In 1324 Musa set out on a hajj (pilgrimage) to Mecca in Arabia. His caravan was huge and caused a sensation in the Muslim world. It was made up of over 60,000 people, including 12,000 servants and 80 camels, each carrying 310 pounds (140 kg) of gold. When it entered Cairo, the caravan was led by 500 of Musa's servants dressed in Persian silks, each bearing a solid gold staff.

SEE ALSO

- Gama, Vasco da • Land Transport
- Mercantilism • Silk Road • Trade

CARSON, KIT

CHRISTOPHER "KIT" CARSON, born in Kentucky in 1809, was a trapper, hunter, scout, and Indian agent who had detailed knowledge of the pathways of the southern Rocky Mountains. A slightly built, bowlegged man with a gentle voice, he gained fame as the guide for two well-publicized explorations of the West. Although he fought against American Indians, he was renowned for being sympathetic to their plight. Carson was often the subject of dime novels, which portrayed him as a larger-than-life frontier hero. He died in Colorado in 1868.

Right **Kit Carson served as an officer in the Union army during the Civil War.**

1809
Carson is born in Kentucky.

1818
His father dies.

1823
Carson is apprenticed to a saddle maker.

1826
Runs away to New Mexico.

1828–1842
Works as a fur trapper and hunter.

1842–1846
Guides Frémont's three expeditions.

1843
Marries Josefa Jaramillo.

1853–1861
Is employed as an Indian agent.

1861
Enlists in the Union army.

1864
Subdues the Navajos; fights in Battle of Adobe Walls.

1868
Dies in Colorado.

Kit Carson was the fifth of ten children. Just two years after his birth, the family moved from Kentucky to Missouri. Before Kit reached the age of nine, his father was killed in a freak accident; his death left the family—with so many young children—in difficult circumstances. Young Carson was apprenticed to a saddle maker but found the work tiresome. He left after a few years and joined a wagon train heading for New Mexico.

FRONTIER LIFE

From 1828 to 1842 Carson roamed the West as a fur trapper and hunter. His travels took him to the Rocky Mountains on many occasions, as well as to Arizona and California. In 1835 he and Jim Bridger traveled together to the annual fur trappers' rendezvous along the Green River in Utah. From time to time, he worked as a buffalo hunter, supplying meat to Bent's Fort in southern Colorado.

On his travels Carson learned Spanish and several Indian languages. He gained a reputation as a soft-spoken but tough man who was calm in a crisis. Like many frontiersmen, he married an Indian woman—an Arapaho. They had a daughter, but Carson's wife died when the child was still young. Soon after, Carson fell in love with Maria Josefa Jaramillo, from Taos, New Mexico.

In 1842 Carson took his daughter back to Missouri to live with his family and to attend school. The return trip changed Carson's life. On a steamboat he met John Charles Frémont, who was then leading a government-sponsored expedition to explore the West. Carson agreed to act as guide.

Right **Bent's Fort, built in 1833, became a key stopping point for caravans taking the northern mountain route along the Santa Fe Trail. Charles Bent, one of the brothers who built the fort, and Carson became brothers-in-law by marrying the Jaramillo sisters of Taos, New Mexico.**

The Santa Fe Trail

The Santa Fe Trail stretched from Missouri to Santa Fe, in present-day New Mexico. Santa Fe was a commercial center of northern Mexico. When Mexico won independence in 1821, it lifted restrictions the Spanish had placed on trade with Americans. A Missouri merchant, William Becknell, traced the trail; he traveled for weeks with a train of pack mules laden with goods. Soon other American merchants took the route each year, carrying cloth and manufactured goods to trade for Mexican blankets, animals, wool, and skins. Profits were good enough to offset the costs of a ten-week journey. Taxes paid by the merchants helped finance local government in New Mexico. The Santa Fe Trail continued to be important until the construction of a railroad to New Mexico in 1880.

HEROIC GUIDE

Carson guided three of Frémont's expeditions to the west. The first, in 1842, charted the Oregon Trail along the Platte River to Fort Laramie and then through South Pass. On his return to Missouri, Frémont wrote a favorable report of Carson. Meanwhile, Carson himself returned to Taos to marry Josefa Jaramillo.

In 1843 Carson joined Frémont again. This time the expedition continued past South Pass to the Great Salt Lake and on to the Columbia River. After resupplying, the expedition turned south to explore the Great Basin. Frémont's plan required a dangerous crossing of the Sierra Nevada range in midwinter. Eventually Carson helped guide the party across the mountains. The party rested at Sutter's Fort and then turned back to Missouri by way of a long, southern route. Once again Frémont's official report extolled Carson's knowledge and courage.

Carson was also involved in Frémont's third expedition, which took the explorer to California as the Mexican War (1846–1848) broke out. Carson joined with Frémont in the efforts to win California for America. He carried messages to another column of American troops advancing from the east

Right **The cold, snowy Sierra Madre range on California's eastern edge presented a formidable barrier to Frémont and Carson.**

and guided the troops to California. Soon afterward he returned to New Mexico. He and a colleague traveled to California once more in 1853. They led more than six thousand sheep to Sacramento and sold them at a handsome profit.

INDIAN AGENT

In the same year Carson was appointed Indian agent for northern New Mexico. In his role overseeing land negotiations between the native peoples and the colonial government, he gained a reputation for fairness. When the Civil War broke out in 1861, Carson joined the Union army. After subduing the Apache and Kiowa, he led a combined force of army and American Indian troops against Comanche Indians based in Texas but was unable to secure a victory.

In 1864 Carson fought a campaign against the Navajo Indians. He is alleged to have burned the Indians' crops and forced them on a long march to a reservation. While some accounts charge him with brutality in this campaign, others maintain that he was caught in a dilemma: he was told by the army that the Navajos would have to surrender or be eliminated, and he acted as he did to keep the tribe alive.

After the Civil War, Carson retired owing to ill health. In 1868 he traveled east to take part in a conference about the Ute Indians. A few weeks after he returned to his family in early April, his beloved wife died in childbirth. The following month Carson also died.

Frémont depended on Carson during his crossing of the treacherous Sierra Nevada:

We marched all in single file, trampling the snow as heavily as we could. Crossing the open basin, in a march of about ten miles, we reached the top of one of the peaks to the left of the pass indicated by our guide. Far below us, dimmed by the distance, was a large snowless valley, bounded on the western side, at the distance of about a hundred miles, by a low range of mountains, which Carson recognized with delight as the mountains bordering the coast. "There," said he, "is the little mountain —it is fifteen years since I saw it; but I am just as sure as if I had seen it yesterday."

John Frémont, *Report of the Exploring Expedition to the Rocky Mountains, and to Oregon and California in the Years 1843–'44*

SEE ALSO
- Bridger, Jim
- Frémont, John

CARTERET, PHILIP

ALTHOUGH HE WAS born to a wealthy landowning family, Philip Carteret (1733–1796) spent his life in the Royal Navy. Also known as Philippe de Carteret, he was a bold officer who made two circumnavigations of the globe. In 1767 he undertook a search for new land in the South Pacific and discovered twenty islands in the process. He served England with distinction in the American War of Independence (1775–1783) and by 1794 had been promoted to rear admiral.

Below **During a distinguished career that gained him a reputation as a courageous sailor, Philip Carteret discovered and named twenty South Pacific islands.**

Philip Carteret was born in 1733 to one of the most important families on Jersey in the British Channel Islands. His grandfather had been the first governor of the American colony of New Jersey. Philip entered the Royal Navy at fourteen and worked his way up from midshipman to lieutenant by 1757. Although he inherited Trinity Manor, the family estate, in 1761, Philip chose to remain at sea while his sister Anne ran the estate.

FIRST PACIFIC VOYAGE

From June 1764 to May 1766 Carteret made his first circumnavigation of the world, on HMS *Tamar*. He was part of a Royal Navy expedition to the Pacific under the command of Captain John Byron, the grandfather of the poet Lord Byron. On the outward journey, Byron claimed the Falkland Islands for Britain, much to the annoyance of Spain. However, the Pacific stage of the expedition was disappointing—despite sailing around five thousand miles, the British failed to find undiscovered land.

SECOND CIRCUMNAVIGATION

Nevertheless, within months of Carteret's return to Britain, the Admiralty equipped another Pacific expedition. Captain Samuel Wallis was to command the flagship, HMS *Dolphin,* and for the first time, Carteret had command of his own ship, HMS *Swallow*.

Carteret and Wallis became separated in December 1766 in the treacherous Strait of Magellan. Wallis, wrongly believing the *Swallow* sunk, pressed on for the Pacific.

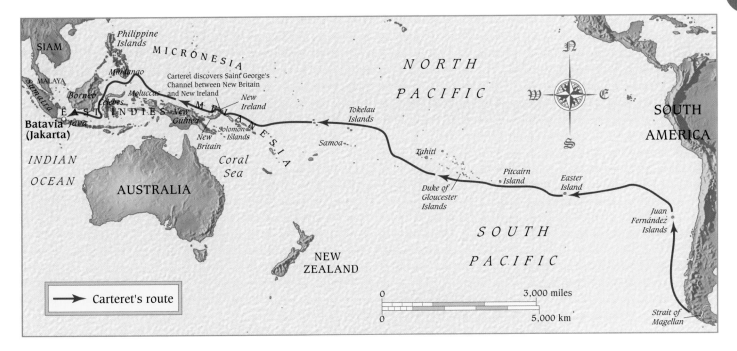

Above **The South Pacific leg of Carteret's second circumnavigation (1766–1768).**

Carteret followed the coast of Chile and then headed west, where, after several months at sea, he found and named Pitcairn Island.

In August 1767 Carteret reached New Britain, first discovered by the British explorer William Dampier in 1699. Carteret realized that New Britain was not a single island but two islands divided by a narrow channel. The names of Carteret's beloved Channel Islands (Jersey, Guernsey, Alderney, and Sark) were given to four islands in the Queen Charlotte group. By November Carteret and his men had come upon twenty new Pacific islands. By the end of 1767, the members of Carteret's crew had been badly weakened by scurvy, and hostile natives were resisting his attempts to land and refresh his store of

The *Swallow*

Carteret's ship was a single-masted sloop of 278 tons (252,196 kg). It carried sixteen guns and on leaving Britain had a crew of 125 men. However, the *Swallow* was over thirty years old and for much of the time had served as a transport ship in the Thames. It had never been on a long sea voyage, and Carteret quickly realized that his ship was unsuited to the task of sailing around the globe. The *Swallow's* rudder was too small for the weight of the ship in heavy seas, and thus, it was difficult to tack to the wind. Even after a larger rudder was fitted, the *Swallow* still needed the help of a boat to pull it around into the wind. By August 1767 it was also leaking badly, and the crew had to man the pumps for the remaining eight months of the voyage.

JANUARY 22, 1733
Carteret is born on Jersey.

1757
Is commissioned a lieutenant in the Royal Navy.

JUNE 1764–MAY 1766
Circumnavigates the world with John Byron.

AUGUST 1766
Sails from Plymouth, England, as captain of the *Swallow*, with Samuel Wallis on the *Dolphin*.

DECEMBER 1766–APRIL 1767
Struggles to get into the Pacific through the Strait of Magellan.

JULY 2, 1767
Discovers Pitcairn Island.

AUGUST 29, 1767
Explores and maps New Britain and New Ireland.

SEPTEMBER 1767
Discovers Portland Island and Admiralty Island.

NOVEMBER 1767
Sick crew spends four months recovering in Dutch East Indies.

MARCH 1769
Carteret brings the *Swallow* home to England after a thirty-one-month voyage.

1777–1783
Sees service in the American War of Independence.

1796
Dies in Southampton, England.

Above **Lying over 1,350 nautical miles (2,172 km) from Tahiti, Pitcairn is one of the most isolated islands in the world.**

supplies. On Egmont Island (present-day Santa Cruz) Carteret's men were attacked after they cut down a palm tree that was sacred to the native islanders.

Sailing west with his injured and dying crewmen, Carteret eventually found a safe harbor at the Dutch colony of Batavia in the East Indies. The *Swallow* limped home in March 1769, ten months after Carteret and his men had been reported lost by Wallis on the *Dolphin*.

After his return, Carteret was promoted, and in the 1770s and 1780s he saw service in both the American War of Independence and the French Revolutionary War. He was especially praised for steering a convoy of damaged ships from Jamaica back to safety in Britain in 1781. By the time he retired in 1794, he had achieved the rank of rear admiral. He died in Southampton in 1796 and was buried in the cathedral in that city.

Discovering Pitcairn Island

After becoming separated from Wallis in the *Dolphin*, Carteret and his crew spent almost ten weeks in the southern Pacific without sighting land. By late June 1767 the *Swallow* was approximately three thousand miles (4,828 km) west of Chile. Carteret offered a bottle of brandy to the first crewman to spot land. The prize was won on July 2, 1767, by a fifteen-year-old midshipman called Robert Pitcairn, stationed high on the mast of the *Swallow*. Carteret named the newly discovered island after the young officer. However, the crew of the *Swallow* was unable to land on Pitcairn because of high seas breaking around the rocks and cliffs that surround the island.

SEE ALSO

- Dampier, William
- Magellan, Ferdinand

CARTIER, JACQUES

THE FRENCH NAVIGATOR Jacques Cartier (1491–1557) explored, named, and described the Gulf of Saint Lawrence on the east coast of Canada. During three voyages to the area, he penetrated the Saint Lawrence River as far as the Lachine Rapids. Cartier's expeditions laid the foundations for future French claims to North American land.

EXPEDITION TO NORTH AMERICA

Not much is known of Jacques Cartier's life before 1534. In that year the king of France, Francis I, decided to send explorers to North America. They were to claim land for France, search for riches, and attempt to find a northwest passage—a sea route that would link the Atlantic and Pacific Oceans and thus provide Europeans with direct access to Asia. Chosen to lead the expedition, Cartier set sail from France on April 20, 1534.

Cartier sailed from his hometown of Saint-Malo in northwestern France with two ships and sixty-one men and landed on the island of Newfoundland about three weeks later. From there he traveled to the Strait of Belle Isle, a narrow passage between Labrador and Newfoundland that connects the Gulf of Saint Lawrence with the Atlantic Ocean. He entered the gulf and encountered a bay on the southwestern coast that he named Baie de Chaleur ("bay of heat"), as its climate was so warm. There, he traded with Micmac Indians, whose amicable relationship with the French continued after this initial contact.

Cartier sailed from the Gaspé Peninsula, skirted Anticosti Island, and saw the mouth of the Saint Lawrence River, to which he returned the following year. On the Gaspé Peninsula he met the Stadaconans, a group of Iroquoian natives from the Quebec area. When Cartier decided that it was time to return to France, he kidnapped two sons of Donnacona, the chief of Stadacona, to take back with him. Cartier was determined to visit North America again and wanted the two boys to learn to speak French so that they might act as interpreters on his next voyage. The two young men did indeed return as guides on Cartier's second trip.

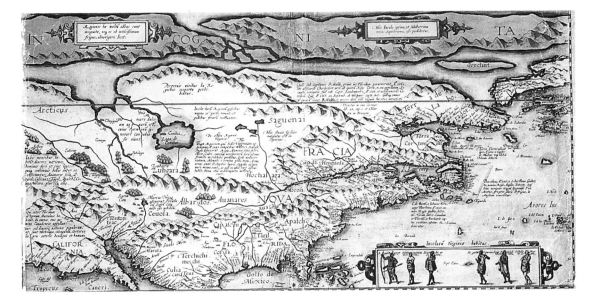

Left **This map, drawn by the Dutch cartographer Cornelius de Jode in 1593, is based on Cartier's own maps. De Jode also attempted to depict interior lakes that Cartier had described only vaguely.**

PROMISE OF RICHES

The report of Cartier's expedition made Francis I eager to find out more about North America, and so he asked Cartier to explore further. On May 19, 1535, Cartier set sail again, this time with three ships. He followed his previous route and then went farther, sailing past Anticosti Island and traveling up the Saint Lawrence River to the Native American villages of Stadacona and Hochelaga (present-day Quebec and Montreal). However, Cartier discovered that further progress up the Saint Lawrence was impossi-

ble, as the Lachine Rapids blocked his way. Cartier's dream of finding a northwest passage to Asia had been dashed.

In Hochelaga, Cartier met American Indians who spoke an Iroquoian language. They told him of the mythical kingdom of Saguenay, which lay to the north of the Saint Lawrence and could be reached via the Ottawa or Saguenay River. Cartier understood that he would find precious metals and spices at Saguenay and was delighted, as these riches would make his expedition a success after all. He returned to Stadacona.

1491
Cartier is born in Saint-Malo, France.

1534
First expedition to North America.

1535
Second expedition to North America.

1541–1542
Final expedition to North America.

JUNE 1542
Cartier meets Roberval in Newfoundland.

1557
Dies in Saint-Malo.

THE LONG, COLD WINTER

No one on Cartier's expedition was prepared for the winter. The temperature dropped well below freezing. The river froze, and there were heavy snowfalls. Crew members began to fall ill with scurvy, and twenty-five men (almost one-quarter of the crew) died of the disease. One of the sons of Donnacona told Cartier that scurvy could be treated with the leaves of the annedda tree, an evergreen similar to cedar or hemlock whose leaves could be crushed and made into a hot drink. Before long, a nearby annedda tree had been stripped bare, and Cartier and his men began to recover.

As soon as the icy river started to flow again, the expedition left Stadacona. On board were several Stadaconans, whom Cartier had kidnapped. Cartier returned to France full of stories of riches and confident he would still find a northwest passage.

A THIRD CROSSING

In 1541 Francis I sent a third expedition to North America but chose not to put Cartier in charge. Instead Cartier was asked to act as guide to Roberval (whose full name was Jean-François de la Rocque, sieur de Roberval). The aim of Roberval's voyage was to set up a base from which to conquer the kingdom of Saguenay.

As Roberval was not ready to go in time, Cartier was sent ahead, under orders of the king, to begin establishing a base. He built a settlement upstream from Stadacona, which he named Charlesbourg-Royal. During a long and harsh winter, Cartier's men killed some local American Indians. In retaliation the Indians killed more than thirty-five Frenchmen. Nevertheless, Cartier was overjoyed to discover the gold and diamonds that the Indians had described to him on his previous visit. In a bid to attack Saguenay, Cartier attempted to transport his army across the Lachine Rapids and up the Saguenay River, but he was unsuccessful because of the difficult terrain and the hostility of the Indians. He decided to return to France and made plans to set sail for home in the spring.

Above **This portrait of Roberval was drawn by Jean Clouet in 1535.**

Jean-François de la Rocque, sieur de Roberval
c. 1500–c. 1560

Roberval was born to a noble family in Carcassone, France. In 1541 Francis I asked him to found a colony in North America, and after some delay caused by financial problems, Roberval set sail. He took with him a group of convicts, with whom he planned to start a colony near Stadacona. However, the venture was not a success. The winter was long, cold, and difficult, and Roberval punished anyone who stepped out of line. He even hanged some convicts for minor crimes. By 1543 he had had enough and returned to France, bringing the remaining colonists with him. According to most accounts of his life, Roberval was murdered as he left a religious meeting in Paris.

BACK TO FRANCE

Meanwhile, in 1542 Roberval reached Newfoundland. When Cartier, too, anchored at the island, he and the expedition leader met up at last, and angry words were exchanged. Roberval demanded that Cartier return to Stadacona at once. Cartier did the opposite of what Roberval wanted and returned to France with his gold and diamonds. However, Cartier was in for a shock. The gold was in fact iron pyrite (also known as fool's gold) and the diamonds were quartz. Both were worthless.

After experiencing his first North American winter, Roberval returned to France with the other colonists. He, too, had failed in the search for riches and for a northwest passage.

Jacques Cartier was sent on no further expeditions. He lived comfortably until his death in about 1557.

CARTIER'S CANADA

On his three voyages to North America, Cartier named many of the places that he discovered. Although most of these names have been long forgotten, some remain. Surviving names include the Gulf of Saint Lawrence and Baie de Chaleur. Several geographical features were named after Jacques Cartier. These names can be found scattered over maps of eastern Canada.

The Tree of Life

*D*uring the winter of Cartier's second voyage to North America, many members of his crew suffered from scurvy. A common disease among sailors on long voyages, scurvy is caused by a lack of vitamin C—found in most fruits and vegetables—in a person's diet. The symptoms are swollen, bleeding gums and wounds that will not heal. In extreme cases scurvy can lead to death. The annedda tree, a tall evergreen, saved Cartier's crew because its needles (leaves) are rich in vitamin C. The tree was later transplanted to Europe, where it was renamed arborvitae, meaning "tree of life."

SEE ALSO

- France
- Northwest Passage

CHAMPLAIN, SAMUEL DE

THE SON OF a naval captain, Samuel de Champlain (c. 1570–1635) was born in Brouage in France. Like many explorers of his time, Champlain was instructed to find a northwest passage around or through the North American continent that would provide European ships with a direct route to Asia. Before his death in 1635 Champlain had explored the Saint Lawrence River, the Maine coast, and the eastern Great Lakes. He firmly established a French hold on Canada, an achievement that earned him the name Father of New France.

Below **Champlain drew this sketch of himself, the only authentic picture in existence, as part of an engraving that depicts the 1609 battle at Lake Champlain.**

VOYAGE TO SPANISH AMERICA

During his twenties Samuel de Champlain fought in the religious wars between French Protestants and Catholics. In 1599 he sought and gained permission from the French king, Henry IV, to take a place on a Spanish ship traveling to the West Indies, Mexico, and northern South America. Reporting to the king on his return, Champlain wrote that "a more beautiful country could not be seen or desired than the kingdom of New Spain."

Jacques Cartier had claimed the Saint Lawrence River for France in the 1530s. The collapse of the first settlements in Canada, together with religious wars at home, had prevented the French from pursuing their claim. In 1603 King Henry IV asked Champlain to join a fur trading expedition to Canada and to reassess "what the colonizers might accomplish there."

EXPLORER

During a scouting expedition up the Saint Lawrence River in 1603, Champlain took the opportunity to explore the Saguenay River. American Indians told him of a large body of water to the north, and he correctly concluded that this water, Hudson Bay, opened to the Atlantic. Continuing along the Saint Lawrence, the party heard of three great lakes to the west. They also explored part of the Richelieu River to the south.

Above **The eastern Algonquin birch-bark canoe, first described by Champlain in 1603, remained virtually unchanged until well into the twentieth century.**

After returning to France, Champlain joined a new expedition led by Pierre du Gua, sieur de Monts, whose aim was to establish a colony. The king had awarded Gua a monopoly on the fur trade in the New World. In 1604, thinking the climate of the Saint Lawrence region too harsh, Gua built his settlement farther south, on the Saint Croix River in present-day Maine. When an early winter and scurvy killed thirty-five of the seventy-nine settlers, Gua moved on and founded a new settlement at Port Royal, Nova Scotia. Between 1605 and 1607 Champlain explored the coast of Maine and as far south as Nantucket Sound.

COLONIZER

In 1608 Champlain was given command of a new campaign to colonize the Saint Lawrence. He established his colony on the site of present-day Quebec. The small group of settlers struggled but survived. For the next twenty years, Champlain labored to build New France. He worked to forge close ties with the Montagnais living in the area. He persevered to establish the fur trade. He sent

c. 1570
Champlain is born in Brouage, France.

1599
Sails to the Caribbean on a Spanish ship, the *Saint-Julien*.

1603
Joins his first expedition to Canada.

1604
Helps to found colonies in Canada.

1605–1607
Explores the Atlantic coast of northeastern America as far south as Nantucket Sound.

1608
Founds Quebec.

1609
Explores and names Lake Champlain.

1615
Maps eastern shore of Georgian Bay.

1615–1616
Carries out final personal explorations.

1629
Loses Quebec to the English.

1633
Returns to Quebec as governor.

1635
Dies in Quebec.

adventurous young Frenchmen to live among Indians and learn their ways and thus become trader's agents or interpreters. The agents not only helped cement the alliance, they also supplied useful information about the region's geography. Champlain hoped they might lead him to the Northwest Passage.

Over the years, Champlain added more and more information to the expanding map of New France. Meanwhile, the colony was growing—although the pace of growth was slow. Champlain also found time to make a couple of exploratory expeditions of his own. Mostly, however, he was consumed by the work of building the colony. On several occasions he had to sail back to France to shore up support for his effort.

Étienne Brulé *1592–1632*

Étienne Brulé, a trader's agent and interpreter of Huron, reached North America sometime in his teens. Champlain came to trust the young man, and in 1610 Champlain persuaded the Hurons to let Brulé live with them. For about the next twenty years Brulé lived as a Huron and passed valuable information to Champlain about the region's geography. Brulé's story ended badly, though. When the British captured Quebec, Brulé and his friend Marsolet were paid by the British to guide them up the Saint Lawrence River to Quebec. When Champlain returned, he was angered by Brulé's treachery. Brulé—perhaps trying to recover his good name—tried to negotiate an alliance between the French and the Seneca, another Indian group. The Seneca, however, were enemies of the Hurons. Interpreting Brulé's action as treachery, the Hurons killed him. According to contemporary sources, news of Brulé's death did not upset Champlain.

Left As Champlain's own engraving shows, the settlement he built at Quebec was more a fortress than a town. In 1608 Quebec's population was twenty-eight; in 1635, the year Champlain died, the population was seventy-six.

Left **Champlain found a large freshwater lake in present-day New York, which he named for himself. Now flanked by farms, Lake Champlain looks quite different from the way it first appeared to the explorer.**

In 1609 Champlain, leading a force of Montagnais and Algonquin Indians on an assault of the Iroquois, came upon a large lake :

The next day we entered the lake, which is of great extent, say eighty or a hundred leagues long, where I saw four fine islands, ten, twelve, and fifteen leagues long, which were formerly inhabited but have since been abandoned because of wars. . . . There are also many rivers falling into the lake, bordered by many fine trees of the same kinds as those we have in France, with many vines finer than any I have seen in any other place. . . . There is also great abundance of fish, of many varieties.

Journal of Samuel de Champlain

SEE ALSO
- Cartier, Jacques
- France
- Jolliet, Louis
- La Salle, René-Robert Cavelier de
- Marquette, Jacques
- Northwest Passage

In 1610 Champlain married Hélène Boullé, who was just twelve years old. Boullé's father was the secretary of the king's household, and by marrying her Champlain may have hoped to gain influence. She joined him in Canada in 1620 and lived there for a few years before returning to France. They had no children.

PROMISE, EXPULSION, AND RETURN

In 1618 Champlain wrote a report proposing the expansion of New France. He persuaded Cardinal Richelieu, one of France's most powerful ministers, to back his vision. Richelieu formed a company of investors and granted them a monopoly in the fur trade on condition that they help colonize New France.

In 1629, a small English force sailed up the Saint Lawrence and captured Quebec. Champlain was sent back to France, where he worked on his final map. When England and France made peace, France regained Quebec. Champlain, named governor, reached New France again in 1633.

In one of his final acts, Champlain sent Jean Nicolet, an interpreter, west. Though Nicolet did not find the elusive Northwest Passage, he set eyes on Lake Michigan and Green Bay—discoveries that laid the groundwork for the French exploration of the Mississippi River Valley. Shortly after Nicolet's return to Quebec, Champlain died.

GLOSSARY

aerial sextant A navigational instrument used to determine the location of an aircraft relative to the earth's surface.

atoll An island consisting of a circular belt of coral with a central lagoon.

aurora borealis An atmospheric phenomenon that causes streaks of colored light to appear in the night sky above the northern polar region.

caliph Title used in various Islamic empires for leaders who trace their descent to the prophet Mohammed.

caravel A small, fast Spanish or Portuguese ship with lateen (triangular) sails.

cholera An infectious, often fatal, disease that causes severe vomiting.

corvette A small eighteenth-century warship, usually with one main deck and one tier of cannon.

curragh An open leather boat with no keel and made of animal skins stretched over a wooden frame; used by the Celts of Ireland and Scotland during the Middle Ages.

dowry Property a woman brings to her husband when they marry.

evangelical Christianity A form of Christianity whose adherents believe in the sole and literal authority of the Bible.

fjord A narrow inlet of the sea surrounded by high cliffs.

forage Food for cattle and horses, such as grasses and hay, usually found or carried by travelers; also, to search for such food.

foundry A factory where metals, especially iron, are smelted and molded into shape.

gangrene A condition, caused by loss of blood supply to an area of the body, that causes the flesh to rot.

glacier A large body of ice that moves slowly down a valley. As a glacier moves, it erodes rocks and soil.

hajj The pilgrimage to Mecca that Islam requires all its followers to make once in their lifetime.

Indian agent A U.S. government official who served as a link with a particular Indian tribe.

iron pyrite A mineral that looks similar to gold but has no value; also known as fool's gold.

mission hospital Hospital built and run by a Christian church group; its aims were to heal the sick and spread Christianity.

missionary school School formed by Christian missionaries, in the Americas, China, or elsewhere, to teach the native inhabitants Western culture and Christian values.

monopoly Total control over the sale of a good or service in a given area.

Oregon Trail A two-thousand-mile path from Missouri to western Oregon used by thousands of settlers moving west from 1841 to the 1880s.

Ottoman Empire Empire of the Turks in western Asia and southwestern Europe, ruled from Istanbul from 1453 to 1922.

outback The wild inland territory of Australia.

polygamy The practice of having more than one spouse.

samurai A member of the warrior class in Japan that was dominant until the late nineteenth century.

scurvy A serious disease caused by lack of vitamin C; its symptoms include bleeding and sponginess in the gums.

sloop A small, light, one-masted warship that usually carried between ten and eighteen cannon.

sultan Title of a secular Muslim ruler, especially of the Ottoman Empire.

tack Change a sailing ship's course by changing the angle of the sails.

wind drift instrument An aerial navigation instrument that calculates the extent to which wind force is causing an aircraft to drift off course.

INDEX

Page numbers in **boldface** type refer to main articles. Page numbers in *italic* type refer to illustrations.

Aerial sextant 121, 159
Africa 114–117
Alaska 87–90
America 129–131
American Indians *see* Native Americans
annedda tree ("tree of life") 153, 154
Antarctica, circumnavigation of 84–86
   expeditions 118–121
   first sighting 85
   mapping 120–121
Arctic 101–103
Atlantic Ocean 104–106, 126–128, 129, 133–134
atoll 85, 159
aurora borealis 101, *102*, 159
Australia 92, 110–112
aviation 103, 118–121

Bellingshausen, Fabian Gottlieb von **84–86**
Bering, Vitus Jonassen **87–90**
Bishop, Isabella Lucy, née Bird **91–93**
Boone, Daniel **94–96**
Bougainville, Louis-Antoine de **97–100**
Boyd, Louise Arner **101–103**
Brazil 133–134
Brendan **104–106**
Brendan's voyage, re-creation of 106
Bridger, Jim **107–109**
Brulé, Étienne 157
Burke, Robert O'Hara **110–112**
Burke and Wills Expedition 111–112
Burton, Richard Francis **113–117**
Byrd, Richard E. **118–121**

Cabeza de Vaca, Álvar Núñez **122–125**

Cabot, John **126–128**, 129
Cabot, Sebastian 127, **129–132**
Cabral, Pedro Álvares **133–135**
Cabrillo, Juan Rodríguez **136–138**
California 136–138, 146–147
caliph 140, 159
camel 139, 141
Canada 126–128, 151–154, 155–158
caravan 126, **139–143**
caravanseries 140
caravel 137, 159
Carson, Kit **144–147**
Carteret, Philip **148–150**
Cartier, Jacques **151–154**, 155
Champlain, Samuel de **155–158**
China 93, 126
cholera 113, 159
circumnavigation of the world 84, 97–99, 131, 148–150
Colorado 92, 93, 145
Columbus, Christopher 126, 127
Company of Merchant Adventurers 132
corvette 84, 159
curragh 105, 159

Da Gama, Vasco 133, 135, 143
Dampier, William 149
Dias, Bartholomeu 133

East Africa 114–117
evangelical Christianity 91, 104–106, 159

Falkland Islands 97, 98
fjord 102, 159
Florida 94, 122–125
Fort Bridger 108
foundry 90, 159
France 97–100, 114, 151–154, 155–158
Frémont, John Charles 145–146
French Revolution 100

Gangrene 138, 159
glacier 102–103, 118, 159
Great Northern Expedition 88–89
Gua, Pierre du, sieur de Monts 156

Hajj 143, 159
Hawaii 92

Îles Malouines *see* Falkland Islands
Incense Trail 139
India 113, 135
Indian agent 144, 147, 159
International Geophysical Year (IGY) 121
iron pyrite 154, 159

Kamchatka 87, 88, 89, *90*
Kentucky 95, 96

Lake Tanganyika 113, 116–117
Livingstone, David 143

Magellan, Ferdinand 130
Mansa Musa 143
mapmaking 102, 120, 130–131
monopoly 142, 158, 159
Mormons 108–109

Napoleon Bonaparte 100
Narváez, Pánfilo de 122, 136
Native Americans 96, 137–138, 147, 156, 157
   in Florida and Texas 123–125
Newfoundland 128, 154
Nile River, source of 115–117
North America 126–128, 129–130, 137–138, 151–154
Northeast Passage 132
North Pole, flights over the 101, 103, 118–120
Northwest Passage 137–138, 156–158
Nugent, Jim (Rocky Mountain Jim) 93

Operation Deep Freeze 119, 121
Operation Highjump 119, *120*, 121
Oregon Trail 108, 109, 146, 159
Ottoman Empire 140, 159
outback 111, 159

Padrón Real (Royal Map) 131
Peter the Great 89

Pitcairn, Robert 150
Pitcairn Island 150
polygamy 109, 159
postal service, first transatlantic 121

Quebec 151, 152, 156, 157, 158

Roberval, Jean-François de la Roque, sieur de 153, 154
Rocky Mountains 92, 107–109, 144–147
Royal Geographical Society 91, 93
Russia 84–86, 87–90, 132

Salt Road 139, 142
samurai 93, 159
Santa Fe Trail 145
scurvy 89, 111, 149, 152, 153, 156, 159
Severin, Tim 106
shipbuilding, in the East 90
Siberia 87–90
Silk Road 139
sloop 149, 159
South America 130–132
South Pacific 85, 148–150
Spain 122–125
Speke, John Hanning 114–117
Spice Route 139
Stadacona 151, 152, 153, 154
Swallow, HMS 148, 149, 150

Tahiti 99
Texas 122–125

Vespucci, Amerigo 129, 135
Vostock 86

Willoughby, Sir Hugh 132
Wills, William John 111–112
wind drift instrument 121, 159

Young, Brigham 109